Daily

MONEY MAIL

MOVES

ABROAD

EVERYTHING YOU NEED TO KNOW
ABOUT LIVING OR WORKING OVERSEAS

Edited by Margaret Stone

Written by Wayne Asher and James Hopegood

KOGAN
PAGE

YOURS TO HAVE AND TO HOLD
BUT NOT TO COPY

First published in 1998

Kogan Page Limited
120 Pentonville Road
London N1 9JN

British Library Cataloguing in Publication Data

A CIP record for this book is available from the British Library.

ISBN 0 7494 2587 3

Typeset by Saxon Graphics Ltd, Derby
Printed and bound in Great Britain by Thanet Press Limited,
Margate, Kent

CONTENTS

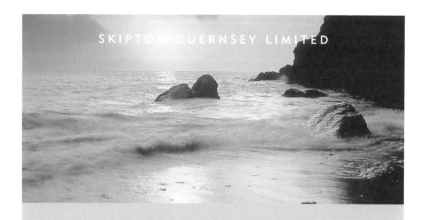

High interest
with no tax deducted

High rates of interest, backed by the solid reassurance of one of the UK's top building societies, is a combination that investors find attractive. With the added benefit of interest paid gross, it's an investment opportunity that's almost irresistible.

So, whether you want instant access to your money, are prepared to give notice or even invest for a fixed term, you'll find just what you are looking for at Skipton Guernsey Limited.

For details of our current interest rates,

Call Now 01481 727374

alternatively, fax us or simply drop us a line!

SKIPTON
GUERNSEY LIMITED

PO Box 509, Canada Court,
Upland Road, St Peter Port,
Guernsey GY1 6DS
Telephone: 01481 727374 Fax: 01481 727440
International contact numbers:
Telephone: +44 1481 727374 Fax: +44 1481 727440

INVEST FIVE MINUTES HERE AND ENJOY YEARS OF SAFE RETURNS.

At Halifax International (Jersey) Limited, we have a range of offshore accounts. There are tiered interest rates, flexible income options, and all interest is paid gross with no tax deducted at source. You can make transactions simply and safely, via telephone and fax, with our International Direct service.

So if you are looking for higher returns without high risks, nothing could be easier. Simply send us the coupon. By return.

HALIFAX INTERNATIONAL
TELEPHONE: 01534 59840
FAX: 01534 59280

For full details of Halifax International (Jersey) Limited please complete the coupon below and send to: Halifax International (Jersey) Limited, PO Box 664, Halifax House, 31-33 New Street, St. Helier, Jersey, Channel Islands JE4 8YW.

Title (Mr/Mrs/Miss/Ms)_____ Initials_____

Surname_____ D.O.B._____

Address_____

_____

Country_____

Postcode_____

Nationality:

☐ UK National
☐ Other (please specify)

_____

Date_____

HALIFAX

INTRODUCTION

IT WILL be a momentous year for many Britons, the men and women who during the course of the next twelve months, will move abroad. It could be to a modest holiday home in the south of Spain or to take up a lucrative contract in Singapore. Either way, after the first excitement of making the decision to leave the country, whether permanently or as part of a career move, the questions will start flooding in. Where shall I live? What shall we do about the children? What happens if I have an accident when I am abroad? Am I really prepared to spend my retirement in a foreign country? Many of these questions only you can answer. It is a very serious step to uproot yourself from your home in the UK to another country, another culture, another climate and another language.

But once the decision has been taken in principle, the move abroad can be one of the most exciting events of your life. But like all such events, the more pre-planning you can do, the better will be the end result. For example, if you are planning to retire abroad to France, you don't need to make a snap decision. Look at not just your favourite region in France, look at the neighbouring areas. The price for a similar property might be considerably cheaper but the amenities just as desirable.

Do you have to move there straight away? You might find

it preferable to rent a home in the area first to find out if it really does come up to your expectations. And you should certainly never be tempted by a bright, seductive house in the sun without first of all seeing it in the driving rain and with the mistral blowing. In other words, take the same care about buying a property abroad as you would about buying your home in the UK.

Buying a home overseas is certainly one of the most important aspects of living abroad. But there are many other considerations as well. You need to be very clear in your own mind about your actual status in the country of your choice, and to know how you stand in respect of the taxman, both at home and abroad. Keeping on the right side of the taxman, wherever he resides, is one of the most important pieces of advice that anyone should heed.

In fact, all the aspects of your personal financial planning that you have undertaken in the UK should be replicated when you pack your bags and move to another country, either on a permanent or a temporary basis. Your investment opportunities may be greater – expatriate earnings can be higher and UK tax liabilities might not loom as large – but you will still need to consider your long-term future. In particular, you will need to look at your pension arrangements.

And the final question which must be asked is: what happens when you want to come back home?

Money Mail Moves Abroad is designed to answer all the queries that you might have starting with when you first consider working or moving abroad right through to the days when you return for the last time to the UK. The text was written and researched by Wayne Asher, who has written on investment for several years, and has lived and worked abroad, primarily in Latin America, and by James Hopegood, who is an authorative writer on pensions and house purchase, whether at home or abroad. And speaking personally as someone who is in the throes of planning a property purchase in France, I hope that you will find this book as helpful as I have done in its making.

Acknowledgements

The authors would like to thank the following for their help in preparing the text: Maurice Fitzpatrick, of accountants Chartrey Vellercatt, Bill Blerim of accountants Blackstone Franks, and Simon Conn of Conti Financial Services.

MANAGING YOUR RETIREMENT

For the expatriate, retirement planning can be very complicated. Can you protect yourself from exchange rate changes? What's the best way to handle your UK pension fund in the light of new legislation? How can you create tax efficient income?

Siddalls can help you make the most of your retirement assets. Our independent financial services cover international investment management including advice on French-based investments, tax and inheritance planning and stockbroking. Because we understand both French and British systems, we can help you keep your options open against a possible return to the UK.

With offices in Bordeaux, Nice and in the UK, we are on the spot to respond immediately to your needs.

If you live in France or you plan to move here, talk to us without obligation on 05 56 34 75 51 *(Bordeaux)*, 04 93 80 40 21 *(Nice)*. Or call us in the UK on 01329 288641.

Siddalls International

Parc Innolin, 3 rue du Golf, 33700 Bordeaux - Mérignac, France Tel: (33) (0)5 56 34 75 51 Fax: (33) (0)5 56 34 75 52

Personal · Investment · Authority

John Siddall International Limited is regulated by the Personal Investment Authority

INTERNATIONAL FINANCIAL ADVISERS AND INVESTMENT BROKERS

1

MOVING ABROAD – GETTING PREPARED

MOVING abroad is a big step and fitting in when you arrive there can be a bigger one still. How to approach it depends a lot on the preparations you make. If you are retiring to the sun, this will be something you have considered for a long time and have probably been loosening your connections with the UK over the years, and spending more and more time in your new country. If a sudden proposition comes your way from your employer, however, you may not have much time to consider the move at all.

Even for seasoned travellers, actually living abroad can be a massive culture shock. Things will be done differently, and it will be you that's out of step. Worse still, you may not even understand what they're saying. It is difficult to stress how different this total immersion can be. There are millions of little things all done differently abroad to at home. Nothing will work as you expect it to, and the cumulative effect of it all can be trying.

In many countries the phones sound different, the cities

are noisier, the middle class tend to socialize in hotels rather than bars, yet nights can be oddly quiet as the main meal is taken at midday not in the evening, while family ties are all-embracing in a way which is not true in the UK. And in some countries domestic staff are cheap to hire.

All this means that making sense of living abroad also depends a lot on you, and before you consider it, you need to ask yourself some searching questions. Be honest with yourself here, you're not out to deceive anyone else.

To some extent, going abroad for a short time as part of your job is the easy way of coming to terms with all this. A spell abroad should give your career a boost, and the company will be able to help with preparations and the daily hassle of foreign existence. But only to some extent.

A married man posted abroad faces some tough choices: what is the best thing to do about the children's education? Send them to boarding school in the UK? Or look for an English language school abroad? More importantly still, how will his wife see it? There can be problems if the wife has a career of her own. A great career opportunity for you may look very different to her – and it is usually that way around, incidentally. She may have to give up her career as part of the move. In the worst case scenario, as in some Middle Eastern countries, she may find it hard to get work and end up being reduced to housewifely status. Boredom sets in and wrecked marriages can easily result. Some employers do not take this sort of thing sufficiently into account.

You also will have to acclimatize quickly and under the pressure of getting a job done, and while you are doing that, your partner will have to sort out a lot of day-to-day aggravations.

WHAT'S IN A CONTRACT?

If you go abroad to work for a UK company, you will get a separate contract of employment. This needs to be considered carefully, something which is especially true if you are working for a new company, perhaps after being head-hunted or through replying to job advertisements. Even before you get to this stage, however, you should find out what briefings and help you will be offered. Many employers will pay for you and your partner to spend several days at one of a number of specialist centres, of which the best known is the Centre for International Briefing, in Farnham, Surrey (see Appendix). This will provide a comprehensive introduction to what living in your new country is really like.

The company should be able to sort out – or at least help with – permits. In the EU you do not need a work permit, but do need a residence permit. Elsewhere the rules are much tougher, and in particular, your partner may not automatically be given a work permit just because you've got one.

When you get your contract, these are the ten major points to watch.

- First things first. Is the contract in English? If not, get it translated, and make sure that it is written down that the English translation is the valid one.

- How much cash are you being offered? Does it cover the fact that your partner may have to give up her career to move with you? Many expatriate postings are essentially hardship postings so you want something to compensate you for this.

■ Check that the salary you are offered really will go further than it would do in the UK. A 10 per cent wage
increase, for example, will leave you poorer than you
would be in the UK if you are sent to Tokyo. There are
a number of sources of information about this: The
Women's Corona Society (see Appendix) produces
'notes for newcomers' at £5 a copy. As an aside, some
countries have attempted to maintain an artificially
high exchange rate, and this can make unlikely countries very expensive for periods of time. Argentina has
sometimes fallen into this category, as have the former
French colonies in West Africa.

■ In what currency will you be paid? You do not want to
be paid in the local currency if it is unstable. This is
because a severe depreciation of that currency against
sterling can reduce your real wealth. Unstable currencies, a category which covers almost all Third World
currencies, are usually associated with countries where
there are exchange controls in force. In such a country,
you may end up having money blocked. So be paid in
sterling. Avoid perfectly sound currencies such as the
US dollar or the Deutschmark if you plan to return to
the UK – this is because you will be taking a currency
risk, and converting currencies counts as a chargeable
event for capital gains tax purposes.

■ You will not need most of this money, so have part of it
paid into your offshore bank account (see your bank
about this). You will probably avoid UK taxation this
way if you are non-resident, and the country where
you live will not really be able to tax you on this sum
even if it wanted to.

- Who will you really be working for? Your company? Or a foreign subsidiary? Make sure that in the event of any dispute the legal system of England (or Scotland) will apply, and make sure that you have access to independent advice. If you are offered work by a firm of which you have never heard, make some enquiries. Do a search at Companies House (see Appendix) in London, and use contacts in the trade to learn more. There have been a number of scandals involving job-hungry expatriates, usually with the payment of up-front fees in return for the promise of work.

- Does the contract spell out your responsibilities and duties in detail? Does it address the fact that working conditions abroad are often very different from those in the UK? And if so, is this reflected in the salary? Take a job in the United States, for example, and you may get considerably less holiday allowance than you would accept in the UK.

- Does the contract spell out what extra you will be offered in the way of perks, pension, removal expenses, accommodation, allowances towards children's education, flights home during leave, or terminal bonus?

- What about renewing your contract? Will it be on the same terms, or will your boss be allowed argue that your initial contract included money to cover one-off removal and dislocation expenses? You also need to get some idea of what will happen to you career-wise upon your return to the UK.

- Are all your concerns dealt with in the contract? If not, get them sorted out in writing before signing. Don't rely on verbal assurances – the person who made them may not have the authority to do so, and may subsequently deny having made them.

CHILDREN'S EDUCATION

If you have children, what to do about schooling will be one of the worst headaches facing you if you are sent abroad for a year or two, and no solution will be really ideal. There are essentially three options:

(1)   Pay for boarding school in the UK.

(2)   Send your child to a British school abroad.

(3)   Use local schooling abroad.

Boarding school in the UK is a common choice, but has several drawbacks. Many children do not take to what is a complete revolution in schooling, and worse still, they may feel they have been dumped while you pursue a career abroad.

The big plus about keeping your child at school in Britain is that the school will be following the National Curriculum, and your child will emerge with UK qualifications. It is expensive, however, and school fees tend to increase faster than the rate of inflation. According to the Independent Schools Information Service (ISIS) (see Appendix), this is what boarding school fees looked like last year. And these figures are per term, not per year.

■   Junior preparatory (ages 7–13) – £2,000–£3,000

■   Senior (ages 13–18) – £2,500–£4,000

ISIS warns that extras can easily add 10 per cent to these costs. You need to make sure than your salary will more than cover these costs, otherwise going abroad will be a losing proposition. The best senior private schools may also require your child to have passed the common entrance examination. For comprehensive information on private education, write to ISIS.

You must also consider what will happen in the school holidays: someone will have to escort them to and from airports, and the school will probably require you to appoint a UK guardian, who really should be a close relative.

A final point: if you are abroad for two to three years, you may find your child still has several years to complete in private school and switching from the private to the state scheme can be seriously traumatic, unless there is an established sixth form college system. Can you afford to pay fees when you return? As a general rule, children benefit from the widened horizons that a spell overseas brings, although the younger they are, the easier such a move is. Making that switch when children are in the middle of the GCSE or A Levels can be fraught with difficulties. Many countries have British schools which follow the National Curriculum, although, again, these will be expensive. There are also American schools where teaching is in English, but the curriculum will be geared to US requirements. The best source for information on this is the European Council of International Schools (see Appendix).

The final alternative would be to enrol your child in the local state system abroad. This is a limited option, available only if you are moving to a fairly advanced country where educational standards are high and classes are taught in English. This could be ideal, but remember that discipline in schools abroad may be much more rigidly enforced that it is in the UK these days.

A final, obvious, but easily overlooked point – what do your children think? What would they prefer? Remember that some options suit some children but not others.

MEDIUM-TERM PREPARATIONS

The obvious one comes first – learn the language. If you are going to live abroad, you will not get the most out of your experience, and will not be respected or taken as seriously if you have not made the effort to learn the language. Reliance on English may be tolerable if you are going somewhere for a year or so but if you're planning to retire abroad it is foolish in the extreme. Failure to learn a language is tantamount to saying that it doesn't matter, and, by implication, neither does the culture of the land where you'll be living. Start to learn something about its history and traditions too, it will all help enrich the experience.

This isn't just moralizing, it's a very practical concern: how will you explain what's wrong to a doctor in an emergency? He or she won't necessarily speak English. What about the plumber? And the bureaucrats at the town hall or the electricity company?

A tip here for the wise expatriate – the best help towards learning a language is motivation. If you have a strong personal reason for learning, you'll do much better than learning because you somehow feel that, in the abstract, it is a good idea.

CHECKLIST

■ See your bank manager to arrange the opening of an offshore account and to get recommendations about banks where you are going. When you have opened your account, arrange how you will deal with it.

■ Tell the taxman you are leaving Britain; ask for form P85 (see chapter 5). At the same time, send your P45 to your tax inspector – you may be entitled to a tax rebate.

■ Find yourself a financial adviser – if you do not have one, call IFA Promotions on 0117 971 1177 which will give you a list of those in your area. As tax is a major consideration abroad, you may prefer to use an accountant instead. Accountants regulated by the Institute of Chartered Accountants are allowed to give financial advice, in any case.

■ Ask the Law Society (see Appendix) for a list of English lawyers with offices abroad. Tell your own solicitor about your plans and discuss the legal implications. You may even want to consider giving him or her power of attorney over your affairs here, especially if you have elderly relatives. Get your lawyer to store valuable documents, such as deeds to property.

■ Consider private medical insurance for you and your family while abroad. For those retiring abroad it is essential; for working expatriates it depends on what deal you and your family are being offered. Falling ill is another good reason for learning the language, incidentally.

■ Talk to your insurance company at home about your property here. You should tell them that you are no longer occupying it. Even though it is being rented out, you may have to pay a higher premium.

- Go to the dentist for a thorough check-up, ditto the doctor, ditto the optician if you wear glasses. Get copies of your medical records and details of prescriptions, and if necessary, have them translated.

- Arrange with your social security office to pay Class III National Insurance contributions if you are likely to return to the UK. These cost £6.05 a week and maintain your rights to the state pension and some other benefits.

WILLS

Everyone should make a will – not doing so often causes heartache to your surviving relatives, Yet surprisingly, two out of three adults in this country never make a will.

Without a will, your property will be divided up according to law, which may not be the way you would have preferred. Unmarried couples, for example, can inherit nothing without a will, and you will lose the chance to leave anything to charity by not doing so.

The period before you go abroad is a busy and hectic time, but if you have not yet made a will, now is the time to do so. Unless your affairs are particularly complicated, you are unlikely to have to pay more than around £60 in legal fees for this.

If you are retiring abroad, you should make a separate will for your assets in that country, although remember that in some European and Latin countries, you cannot cut out a surviving spouse and children from your will. Whatever your will says, they will be entitled to a cut of the estate.

If you are trying to shed your English or Scottish domicile, then your main will should be in the country where you live; to have your main will in the UK could be taken as a sign that you have not really severed your connections with Britain.

2

FINDING AND BUYING YOUR PROPERTY

THE DECISION to up sticks, leaving family and friends to live and work abroad, is never one taken lightly. Moving house, even within the 5-mile radius that most of us change home, is one of the most stressful activities there is. A move to a foreign country with different laws, customs and usually language can be fraught with difficulties.

This is never so true as when it comes to picking out the property you want to buy and turn into your home. How to find it can be hard enough in itself, but then you have to negotiate with local vendors, possibly local lenders as well and solicitors. All this can be a minefield, and it will be particularly difficult for those who do not have a reasonable command of the language.

Once you have chosen and bought your home overseas, you then have to get there. The expense and hassle will be largely related to how many of your personal possessions you want to take with you out there. Obviously, a couple retiring to the sun for good are far more likely to want to take as many of their belongings as possible with them than someone going overseas to work for a couple of years. But either way, possessions must be packed, insured and transported.

WHERE TO FIND YOUR OVERSEAS PROPERTY

Whether you are working or retiring abroad, the first thing you need is somewhere to live abroad. The UK's culture of property ownership may well mean that you are not prepared to rent your home. Instead, you will want to buy it outright. Finding your dream home can be a tricky task, but there are many people and organizations who can help you here. You must find a home you are happy with to live in and be sure it does not hide a host of hidden extra costs that will burden you for years to come.

While many people first conjure up the idea of buying a home overseas when they are on holiday, in reality, few of them have the good fortune to fall in love with their dream home while they are there. And that is probably just as well. There are enough incidents of families, full of holiday euphoria, being tempted to buy property from timeshare touts and entering into irrevocable commitments which they later regret, but cannot undo. For most, finding a home when moving overseas means an immense amount of work. Foreign property information is available from a wide number of sources. These can be the local estate agents you visited on holiday, national newspaper advertisements and specialist magazines such as *Living in France* which mainly target property buyers.

However, the first port of call for many househunters looking to buy abroad is one of the exhibitions organized to promote firms involved in selling properties abroad. Often these exhibitions are put together by the many specialist magazines that cater for the needs of UK residents moving abroad. Two of the major exhibitions are organized by magazines *World of Property* and its rival publication *Homes Overseas*.

Homes Overseas usually has two exhibitions a year in February or March and October. The first one in 1998 will be at the NEC in Birmingham. Admission is free and along with the usual agents and property developers there are stands offering free legal and financial advice. *World of Property* runs up to three exhibitions a year in March, May and September in either Manchester or Sandown, Isle of Wight. Entrance costs £2.50 per person and there are some 120 exhibitors representing 15 countries.

In addition to these magazines and their showcases, there is a host of other publications that can give you help in finding your property abroad. As well as advertising homes for sale, they also have articles giving advice and hints on how to do it. These are available in large newsagents. Popular titles are *Homes Overseas*, *Foreign Property News*, *Overseas Property Match*, *International Property*, *Spanish Property News* and *French Property News*.

Sources of information are more immediately available from magazines like *Exchange & Mart* and *Dalton's Weekly* – publications simply listing items for sale ranging from cars to fridges to properties to collectors' items. Both magazines will be found on just about any newsstand.

Many major property developers in the UK have big interests overseas and they are only too keen to sell to Britons wanting to live abroad. They will offer a selection of different types of homes, from part-owned holiday lets, to flats and houses. A lot of the time these developers build properties in areas they know are already favoured by UK expatriates and will tailor the deals they offer accordingly. For example, Taylor Woodrow has a number of developments in Spain. It not only sells you the property, but in order to reel you in as a prospective buyer, it will offer help on where to find reputable English-speaking lawyers and other specialists who can help you. Other UK property developers building overseas are Bovis and Wimpey.

LOOK BEFORE YOU LEAP

Do not buy a property off the page sight unseen. An attractive photograph of a villa in Spain is unlikely to show the open sewer over to the left near the beach, the fact that there are no foundations and a hotel complex is being built at the rear. An air fare and the cost of a hotel for a week or two to check out both your new home and the surrounding area it is in will be a very good investment indeed.

When you are doing this, you must think about what amenities you will need living there, both now and in the future. Going native living in the middle of nowhere may sound attractive and your dream home may look great on a hot sunny day. But what is it like in winter?

There are a number of important questions to ask yourself before making that big commitment.

- Are the roads passable off season when you may not have visited? Will they be gentle with your car if you intend to drive and, just as importantly, are local driving habits gentle too?

- How good is the local transport? Does the public

transport system stop in winter? This is often the case as some tourist resorts become ghost towns for the winter months and vital amenities such as buses simply stop running or, at the very least, run a very limited service.

- Can you be connected cheaply and easily to mains gas, electricity and water supplies? Having to ship any of these essentials in or having them specially connected up could be both expensive and take time to achieve. However, don't forget that in many rural areas of Europe, bottled gas is the norm.

- If the house is not on the telephone, how long will it take to get connected? If you are thinking about living in an isolated area with few nearby English speakers this should be a very big consideration.

- What are the local healthcare facilities like? If you are retiring overseas this is very important. Similarly, if there is a local doctor on call, does he or she speak English? If you are taking out private medical insurance to cover you abroad it is worthwhile asking your insurer about local hospitals and other medical facilities.

- What are local schools like? For those working abroad with families, you could find difficulties finding a suitable school place for your child if you choose to live in an area with a very small or no foreign community.

- What about amenities? How far away are the local shops? The 3-mile drive down twisty roads might seem fun when you are on holiday, but do you really want to make this journey every day for your daily bread? You may find, however, that local residents buy from local delivery services. Other essentials to check are where the nearest post office is and also the local police station and pharmacy.

OLD VERSUS NEW

Falling in love with a tumble-down farmhouse may be a wonderful idyll, but its practical implications can be serious. Buying an old farmhouse has its plus points. There are likely to be few planning problems, you could end up with a very lovely, individual home of great character, and the limited number should mean they are easy to sell.

But old homes may be badly built, connection of services may be shaky at the very least, alterations can be very complicated and repair bills can be sky high. Ask yourself these questions:

- Do you want to live in the country all year round?

- Are you proficient at D-I-Y?

- Are you prepared to face up to the fact that cost of any renovation will almost certainly escalate?

- Will you be around, or be able to make fairly frequent trips, to oversee work on the property?

Buying a new home has its advantages. New villas and apartments are often well built and easy to sell. Apartments in particular can have good security systems and low running costs and are cheap to maintain. But they may be cursed by poor foundations. Villas may be expensive to keep up particularly if they have big gardens, and they can be noisy if they are in tourist areas and are near other homes rented out on holiday lets.

YOU NEED PROFESSIONAL HELP

Once you have found a home you are happy to buy and think will suit your purposes now and in the future, it is crucial you get proper advice from people who are qualified to give it. It is hard to know which is worse: falling among thieves and being fleeced by sharks on the hunt for unsuspecting victims, or losing just as much time and money because you did not understand what you were doing or got incompetent and amateur advice.

Finding a decent adviser is not as hard as it may first appear. Major lenders operating overseas such as subsidiaries of Abbey National and Woolwich have considerable experience of overseas markets and usually have offices there. They can help you find a reputable lawyer and other professionals who will also speak English. Having an English-speaking professional on your side can help prevent misunderstandings and frauds. In the same way, major developers and builders with interests overseas should also be in a position to point you in the right direction.

Many independent financial advisers specializing in this area will be of help and there is also a number of UK solicitors such as Bennett & Co and Cornish & Co and accountant Blackstone Franks (see Appendix for details) that concentrate on giving advice to those moving overseas. The Law Society may also be in a position to at least put you in contact with its counterparts overseas who may be able to push you towards good lawyers in those countries.

Unfortunately, there are few associations that can offer a central database. The Federation of Overseas Property Developers, Agents and Consultants (FOPDAC) (see Appendix) was set up in 1973 and it requires its members to comply with a code of conduct and will investigate complaints against its members. FOPDAC members include chartered surveyors, architects, planners, developers, tour operators, travel agents, lawyers, estate agents and builders. Its members operate in many countries including Spain, the Balearic Islands, the Canary Islands, Cyprus, France, Italy, Greece, Malta, Portugal, Switzerland and Thailand.

Solicitors Bennett & Co have a checklist of vital dos and don'ts:

■   Do talk to a British lawyer before you sign anything.

■   Do read any and all small print in anything you are given and get help to work out what it means if you need to.

■   Don't hand over any cash until your lawyer tells you it is safe to do so.

■   Don't let anyone talk you out of getting all the professional advice you think you need and feel comfortable with.

■   Don't make any final decisions you cannot go back on until you get home and have had a good think about it.

LEGAL PROCESS OF BUYING YOUR PROPERTY OVERSEAS

Before you make any irrevocable step, make sure that you are fully aware of the housebuying process in the country of your choice. Your ignorance could cost you money. The rules in mainland Europe are quite different from those in England and Wales. For example, pulling out of an agreed offer is not possible, and nor should the seller be able to indulge in a little bit of gazumping at your expense. And much as we complain about the cost of housebuying and selling in the UK, the fact is that in many other countries the costs are considerably higher.

These are the basic facts you need to have at your finger-tips before making any offer.

- Is the title good?

- Do you make the offer in writing? And by whom (your estate agent or a legal firm)?

- Can you back out having made an offer?

- Can the seller back out?

- Costs – lawyers', estate agent's, and anyone else?

- Is VAT payable?

- Surveys – cash?

- Will there be tax to pay if you sell in the future?

- What are the implications of foreign property on your will?

WHAT HAPPENS IN FRANCE

There are two key professionals you will have to deal with when buying a home in France: the estate agent (although, as in the UK, you may buy direct from the vendor) and the lawyer or *notaire*. An estate agent must have professional qualifications and has to display both his or her annually renewed professional charter and financial guarantee that shows he or she can hold deposits of at least FF500,000 (£52,630) in his office.

The *notaire* is a public servant reporting to the Ministry of Justice. His or her job is straightforward: to ensure that the letter of the law has been followed, the taxes have been paid and generally to make sure that the transaction is valid. Once you have settled on the property you want to buy, you would be advised to have a survey done to make sure that it is structurally sound. Once you have agreed a price, the actual purchase is a two-stage process. But it is important to remember that it is not like the English home-buying process. The first stage where a preliminary contract is agreed is in fact binding and the second document is more for registration.

First stage

There are three types of preliminary contracts for existing properties. Two tie in one party to the sale while one ties both sides in. The *promesse de vente* commits the seller to hand over the property to the buyer at a set price. If the buyer pulls out, then he forfeits the deposit to the seller. This is paid as damages because the seller has been unable to proceed with any other buyers. Often it is for a set period during which the the buyer must confirm he wants to buy. While this contract gives you time to consider the purchase, you may in danger of losing your deposit if you decide not to buy.

The *promesse d'achat* commits the buyer. If he refuses to go ahead with the purchase he will lose his deposit.

The *compromis de vente* or *promesse synalloginatique de vente* ties in both parties and pulling out of it can mean losing the deposit if the contract does not contain *conditions suspensives*. These are terms and conditions that the *notaire* must confirm:

- the seller has legal title to the property

- the mortgage is not higher than the sale price

- any local regulations which may affect you

- any pre-emptive rights, such as charges, on the property.

If any conditions are not met, you get your deposit back and you will also have a month to sort your mortgage out if you have not done so already. At this stage you also pay over your deposit which is usually between 5 and 10 per cent.

Second stage

The second stage is to sign the deed of sale or *acte de vente*. This looks just like the preliminary contract and is drawn up by the estate agent or *notaire*. Once all the legal requirements have been met, the final contract – the *acte authentique* – is signed and witnessed. This done, the process is over.

The original *acte de vente* is left with the *notaire* and if you want to prove title you must get a copy from him or her. You can obtain a confirmed or notarized copy from him or her.

Conditions of owning

You can own your property in two ways and the way you

choose to do it will depend on whether you want your children to get a share of your home when you die. Owning *en division* says that when you die, the property is divided amongst all your heirs. Buying *en tontine* means when you die, your spouse is regarded as having owned the property from the start, so it is not split up with any children.

Costs

You may have to pay the French version of VAT, the *taxe sur la valeur ajoutée*, of 20.6 per cent on the purchase price. But this is waived on any home over five years old. There is also a 5.4 per cent registration tax and a local tax of about 1.6 per cent.

In most cases estate agent charges are paid by the vendor, but do not assume this as along with their fees, it will vary from region to region. The *notaire*'s fees will have to be paid and depend on the value of the property. Here is a rough guide to *notaire*'s fees:

Less than FF20,000 –	2.5 per cent
FF20,000 to FF40,000 –	1.65 per cent
FF40,000 to FF110,000 –	1.1 per cent
FF110,000 to FF800,000 –	0.55 per cent
Over FF800,000 –	0.3 per cent

(*Source*: Blackstone Franks)

Wills

You are well advised to make a will in France in addition to your English one. If you are permanently resident in France your home as well as any other possessions will be dealt with according to French law. Not having a French will may mean your goods are distributed among your children and grandchildren regardless of whether you want that or not.

WHAT HAPPENS IN SPAIN

As in France, a key figure in the property-buying process in Spain is the lawyer or *notario*. His or her job is simply to ensure all legal requirements are fulfilled. You may be paying the fee, but that does not necessarily mean that he or she acts in your best interests. It is a very good idea to retain a separate Spanish lawyer to act on your behalf.

Much criticism has been levelled at the Spanish property market for the way prospective foreign lawyers can lose out. A new change that will greatly help UK buyers is the Collaboration between Registrars and Notaries. This says that before a *notario* can sign off a title deed, he must send it to the Land Registry for a list of charges and liabilities against the property.

The Land Registry returns this and it must be included in the title deed. When this is done the *notario* sends it back to the Land Registry which then registers it in the new owner's name. A word of warning: this does not apply if you make your deeds out before a Spanish consul in a different country.

All Spanish property transactions have to be registered at a public notary with an *escritura de compraventa*, or conveyancing deed. This has to be signed by both the seller and by either you or someone with power of attorney for you. If a couple is buying, then both need to sign. If you ask a representative to act as your attorney they must have permission written in Spanish to do so.

A major point to remember is that if you are buying from someone who has mortgage arrears or has subsequently become bankrupt, his or her creditors may still be able to repossess the property after you have bought it if you have not registered your *escritura* with the Land Registry. Do this immediately and double check it has been carried out properly. For a fee the Land Registry will give you a *nota simple* with the property's details including any arrears.

It can be some months before the sale is officially recognized by the signing of the *escritura*, so doing anything you can to protect your prospective purchase for what can be a considerable time is very wise. Once you have made an offer you do not need any holding contract or *contrato privado*, but it is a very good idea to get one. As well as giving details of the agreed price, the deposit, if one is required as some UK lenders will grant 100 per cent mortgages for Spanish properties although often deposits of at least 20 per cent may be needed, and moving in dates, it is also legally binding and can be used to force the other party to sign an *escritura*. However, it does not stop the current owner from selling it to someone else.

It is also a good idea to take possession as soon as possible. Every transaction needs two searches, at the start and at the end, and although a property may be free of debt at the start, it may not be at the end. Speed lessens the risk.

Since there can be a long gap between agreeing the *contrato privado* and the *escritura* it is also a very good idea to get your lawyer to check nothing untoward has happened in the meantime.

When you finally get to register the deal with the Land Registry, it will then return the *escritura* to you with its official stamp and reference number. The *escritura de compraventa* is now the *escritura publica* – the title deed. The property is now yours, but it is still advisable to get the document properly translated into English so you can check it.

Wills

You do not need to make a separate will in Spain, but it is advisable to do so. As an expatriate, Spanish law will allow your Spanish property to be covered by your English will. But it means being probate in both England and Spain which is not only time-consuming but costly too. A Spanish will help solve these problems.

Costs

Not only do lawyers cost money, but Spain levies both national and local taxes and these can be a burden. Take care: the authorities are clamping down on tax avoidance.

The *notario* charges according to the property's value and the costs are split between the buyer and seller, although usually the buyer agrees to pay it all.

Your own lawyer charges about 4 per cent of the price of your new home. Some of the taxes you pay depend on who you buy from. If you buy from a private individual there is a 6 per cent transfer tax, but no VAT. But buying from someone like a property developer incurs a 15 per cent tax for the plot of land and 6 per cent for the building itself. The *plus valia* is an urban property tax on whatever capital gain the local council feels has been made. The seller is officially responsible for this, but as it is attached to the property itself, the buyer often pays it.

Do not to be tempted to have an official and an unofficial price to avoid tax. The Spanish taxman is on the case and will sting you for it eventually.

The total you will pay in fees and taxes, including Land Registry charges, will be about 10 per cent of the property value. Don't forget other local taxes and any costs involved in connecting up utilities.

WHAT HAPPENS IN PORTUGAL

Leasehold ownership of private homes does not really exist in Portugal; property is owned on a freehold basis – *propriedade* (ownership) *livre de quaisquer onus ou encargos* (in full right). If anyone offers to sell you a leasehold property, it is time to smell a rat.

As in France and Spain, a privately appointed lawyer, as opposed to the public notary who checks all is in legal order, can be your best friend. But make sure your lawyer is reputable and is not acting for the seller. Good estate agents can be contacted via the Portuguese Chamber of Commerce (see Appendix).

The tax situation in Portugal can be desperately complicated and some UK lenders willing to grant mortgages overseas such as Abbey National insist that homes be bought through offshore companies set up in Gibraltar, Jersey, Guernsey or the Isle of Man.

After you have decided on a property, step one is to get your lawyer to check it out at the Land Registry. Most Portuguese properties are now registered, so this should not be a problem and this should ensure the title is genuine.

When you make an offer you will be offered one of two

preliminary contracts: a straightforward 'Option to purchase' or the far better promissory contract of purchase and sale – *contrato-promessa de compra e venda*. With an option to purchase you simply buy the right to buy the property. Although it costs nothing to set up this contract, any cash you may have handed over could disappear at the end of the offer period, and even if you buy, it may not be taken into account in the purchase price.

The promissory contract is a far better deal as it is legally binding, laying out the conditions of both buying and selling. The contract is signed by both parties at the public notary's office where the property will be finally bought.

If the seller does not keep his or her end of the contract you can get twice your deposit back. This could be a lot of money – deposits are about 10 per cent. If you renege on the contract you could just lose the deposit you have already paid.

Your lawyer should check who holds the title to the land or property you are buying and whether it is mortgaged or not, along with any other clauses or charges on the property.

The process ends when you and the seller sign the *escritura pública de compra e venda* (sale and conveyance deed). The *escritura* is signed in front of the local *notario* or notary in the same way as it is in Spain. If you are unable to do so in person, you can give someone power of attorney to do it, but you should make sure the permission is written in Portuguese. The *notario* cannot sign you off as the new owner until he or she has seen a number of key documents:

- a certificate from the local Land Registry

- a certificate from the *Repartição de Finanças* – the Portuguese taxman – usually the *caderneta predial*

- if the property was built after 1951 you will need a habitation certificate, which also makes it easier to get things like electricity put in

- proof you have paid your SISA or property transaction tax

Buying your home in Portugal will be costly and it is a good idea to put aside perhaps 20 per cent of the house value to cover your expenses. The registry and notary fees will be about 3 per cent while the SISA is 10 per cent, although there are some exemptions available.

There is also the *Mais Valias* or capital gains tax to be paid on properties bought after the start of January 1989. Half the profit made is assessed as taxable income and the rates vary between 16 per cent and 40 per cent.

Wills

You do not need to make out a separate Portuguese will as, like Spain, if you are a foreign resident your home is covered by your English will. But it is still a very good idea to make one out, as again it solves the expensive problem of having to apply for probate in two separate countries.

TIMESHARE PROPERTY

Timeshare is in theory a good idea, allowing people to buy weeks in the sun, which can be exchangeable for other weeks around the world, for a lot less than it would take to buy a villa of your own. Over 300,000 Britons are now reckoned to own timeshare weeks, and major corporations with reputations to defend are now entering the timeshare business.

However, timeshare has a poor reputation, mainly because of the antics of unscrupulous developers, who seek to cover their costs quickly by using high pressure sales techniques on unsuspecting tourists lured to 'presentations' and 'awards ceremonies'. Some people are then lured into buying accommodation that they do not want, or is not as they were promised. Many are the stories of people who were sold an apartment which overlooked the sea, when in reality it overlooked the town dump and was above a noisy disco. That these techniques do work is testimony to the power of professional selling and also the sad fact that carefree holidaymakers in the sun will do things they would never consider at home without consulting a lawyer.

The international nature of the business makes it more difficult to stand up for your rights in the case of a dispute. However, the key problem is that you do not automatically enjoy the right to a cooling off period, a period in which you can think again after the sales hype has worn off, and cancel if you want to. Britain does have this provision – the Timeshare Act, passed in 1992, gives people a 14-day cooling off period – and when it became law, timeshare hustlers vanished overnight from these shores. Partly under pressure from Britain and Germany, whose nationals were among the main victims of timeshare touts in Spain, the European Commission ordered all member states to change their own laws to provide for a 10-day cooling off period, and do so by 19 April 1997. Britain has already done so, while Germany, Portugal and Holland did the same. Spain, so far, has not done so. Other laggards include Italy, France and Greece.

If you don't want to buy

If you are pestered by the hustlers and do not want to buy timeshare property, the rule is simple – stand firm:

- Firmly refuse to attend 'presentations', which are often backed up by promises of prizes or awards. Remember that the worst kind of timeshare firms never use the word timeshare at all, but any mention of holiday ownership, to take just one euphemism, means the same thing.

- Ignore the timeshare touts, who also resolutely avoid the word timeshare, and may play on your sympathy in a ploy to get you to attend.

If you are interested

- Do your homework first. The Department of Trade and Industry has a useful booklet, *Your Place in the Sun*, which explains how timeshare works and looks at the pitfalls. It is free from your local Citizens' Advice Bureau. The Timeshare Council also has a free information pack (send SAE) (see Appendix).

- Never, never, under any circumstances, sign anything on the spot, whatever pressures or inducements are offered. Remember that discounts for immediate signing are factored into the price anyway. Instead take the paperwork away and talk to your lawyer back in Britain.

Remember that you get what you pay for. This is important because many people buy timeshare because of the facility to exchange your weeks for others in other resorts throughout the world through RCI. But you won't be able to exchange weeks you bought cheaply at some downmarket Spanish resorts in February for ones in the Lake District or the Alps in spring.

If it's already too late

■   Under British law a contract signed because of a misrepresentation or fraud is void at law. If you paid a deposit, you could probably escape having to pay the balance if you can substantiate your claims that you were duped, but your chances of recovering the deposit are slight.

■   If you paid by credit card, you are protected by Section 75 of the Consumer Credit Act, which makes the card company equally liable. However, you will have to prove your case, and some card companies routinely argue that the Act does not apply to foreign transactions, a view disputed by the Office of Fair Trading. You may have to issue a writ in the small claims court if they prove obdurate.

■   Many timeshare firms have lost their credit card facilities; instead, they may suggest that you take cash out on your card as their machine is temporarily down, and if you do that, you have no protection at all.

■   The Timeshare Council, which represents the reputable timeshare firms, offers a conciliation service for people in dispute with non-members at a cost of £30.

3

MOVING OVER THERE

YOU HAVE settled on a property abroad, thoroughly checked it and then bought it. All that remains to do is to physically move out there. This can be as daunting a part of the whole process as choosing a property in the first place. What to take and what to leave must be decided. Is it cheaper to leave or sell some of your household goods in the UK and buy new ones out there? When you are thinking about this, do bear in mind that not all UK standard electrical appliances are compatible with other goods in the country you are going to live in. If so, it may make more sense to buy a toaster out there.

When it comes to actually moving your possessions, a good deal of help is at hand from removal firms specializing in international deliveries. But there are two points to bear in mind when picking your removal firm:

- If you use a freight forwarding agent, make sure they do not just deliver to a port of entry into your chosen country, leaving you to arrange to get it from there to your home.

- Beware going for the lowest quotation. If it is too cheap, the service may simply not be up to scratch. If the firm destroys any of your property or worse, goes bust, there may be little or no redress.

Make sure any removal firm you use is an overseas member of the British Association of Removers (see Appendix), via the international trade association, the Federation of International Furniture Removers (see Appendix). Also check that the company you use links up with reputable removal firms in the country you are going to – a good service in the UK is no good if it all falls apart when it arrives overseas.

Get several quotes, and make sure that they visit your current premises. Be clear about exactly what you are getting. Find out about their international experience in detail – when did they last move a house contents to where you're going? Ask the firm about customs formalities, and get a date for when everything will arrive. This will depend on how your property is being moved – outside Europe it will go by sea, unless you pay a huge amount extra for it to be shipped as air freight.

Insuring your goods is essential, and all risks cover gives you the best protection. This means you have to work out how much it would cost to replace your property in the case of disaster.

Reputable companies should be able to provide a working knowledge of the country you are moving to, as well as provide refunds and compensation if problems occur. If they are worth their salt, these companies should also be able to deal with overseas customers and quarantine regulations for you.

You yourself can arrange to have your possessions shipped out. This might be particularly attractive if you

have a modest amount of goods to take out. Airlines are happy to take your worldly possessions abroad but at a price, and do bear in mind that it is up to you to ensure that everything is properly packed up and safe. It is possible to fly your goods overseas using a removal firm such as Davies Turner or Pickfords' international remover subsidiary Allied Pickfords (see Appendix). These companies buy space from airlines and shipping firms in bulk, so you should be able to get a better price.

COSTS

How much you pay will depend on a number of variables ranging from choice of destination to whether a delivery firm has a regular run to that destination. Table 3.1 is based on a 3- to 4-bedroom home being emptied to move to a European city from the UK and excludes insurance.

Table 3.1 Costs of moving by road and sea

Destination	Cost
France (Paris)	£3,000
France (Nice)	£3,500 to £4,000
Spain (Madrid)	£4,000 to £4,500
Portugal (Lisbon)	£4,500 to £5,000
Germany (Cologne)	£3,000
Germany (Munich)	£4,000 to £4,500
Italy (Milan)	£4,000 to £4,500
Italy (Rome)	£4,500 to £5,000
Republic of Ireland (Dublin)	£3,000

Insuring your possessions for that one-off journey abroad is also a very sound thing to do. The amount you pay will depend on a number of factors, not least, whether your goods have been packed professionally and are therefore less likely to fall out of the box and be broken!

The split between soft goods – things like carpets – and hard goods – like tables and chairs – will affect the amount you pay for your insurance. Table 3.2 assumes hard and soft goods are split equally, and shows one-off payments for one-off cover.

Table 3.2 Insurance cover by destination, one-off payment

Destination	Amount of cover £20,000–£50,000
France	£250–£625
Spain and Portugal	£500–£1,250
New Zealand, USA, Australia and Canada	£750–£1,875
Argentina	£1,000–£2,500

The premium will cover all risks, but anyone claiming will have to pay 1 per cent of the total sum assured with a minimum of £50 and maximum of £100. The cost is based on length of journey, handling at individual ports and climatic conditions.

FLYING IT THERE

How much you have to pay to ship your household goods out by air will depend on how much it all weighs and how far it has to go. British Airways charges by the kilo and has a minimum freight charge of £33 to all European destinations or £50 world-wide.

There is also a handling charge with a minimum of £14.50 or 5.1p per kilo and shipments to European Community countries attract VAT of 17.5 per cent.

Table 3.3 Costs of airfreight by kilo

Destination	Price per kilo
France	£0.85 to £0.59
Portugal	£2.01 to £1.65
Spain	£1.73 to £0.62
Italy	£2.64 to £2.14
South Africa	£4.50 to £3.00
New Zealand and Australia	£6.97 to £3.97
Canada	£2.44 to £2.35
USA	£5.30 to £1.30
Saudi Arabia	£4.20 to £1.80
Kenya	£3.73
Far East incl. Hong Kong, Singapore, Thailand and China,	£5.41 to £2.51
Argentina	£11.00 to £3.67

4

GETTING A MORTGAGE FOR YOUR PROPERTY ABROAD

NOW YOU have to raise the cash to finance your new home. If you are lucky, your employer will sort it out for you. In most cases this is not the case. So you have a choice: buy with cash if you can, or raise a mortgage.

When buying abroad, as in the UK, cash is king. The more homeowners are able to put down as a deposit, the better off they will be, as the mortgage debt is lower, so monthly payments are lower. Sadly, most people cannot afford to buy their homes outright, so they have to raise a mortgage instead. There are two routes people living and working abroad can go down to finance their house purchases abroad:

- getting a home loan in the UK

- applying for a mortgage from a lender in the country the property is being bought in.

Loans overseas can be organized from either a local company or a subsidiary of a UK lender such as the Abbey

45

National and the Woolwich that specialize in home loans for expatriates or from independent financial advisers such as Conti Financial Services or Blackstone Franks, both of whom specialize in advising expatriates on all aspects of living and working abroad. Blackstone Franks also have a network of partners in a number of foreign countries.

A UK LOAN FOR YOUR OVERSEAS HOME

There are two different ways of using a mortgage raised in the UK to buy a property overseas:

■ use any extra equity in one's present home over and above the value of the existing mortgage to buy another property outright

■ arrange a separate second mortgage.

Most lenders will let homeowners take out a new, bigger mortgage – this is called remortgaging – and use the extra money raised to buy another home.

This is the best route to go down if you possibly can. However, as specialist advisers will tell you, buying a home does not only rely on rational choices. Many clients will say they do not want all their eggs in one basket. They do not like the idea of tying two properties together for fear of losing them both. As a result, they are willing to lose an overseas property if they get into financial difficulties and have their UK property kept safe. This may be understandable, but it does not necessarily make financial sense.

Lenders are keen on this method of buying another home as they do not have to worry about borrowers being able to keep up the payments on two properties. Lenders lose money if they have to repossess a home, so the last thing they want is the danger of having to repossess two properties instead of just one. Having to do this overseas can only bring them further trouble and expense.

From the borrower's point of view there are also big pluses, particularly as borrowers do not need their lenders' permission to let out or make any alterations to their second properties. There is also just one monthly mortgage bill to pay, not two and provided the mortgage is taken out on your main UK residence, you keep your mortgage interest tax relief (which is given at 10 per cent on the first £30,000 of the home loan).

The alternative is to take out a second mortgage to pay for the overseas home. Homeowners unable to remortgage existing properties may have to do this. It can be difficult to get mortgages of more than three-quarters of the value of the property.

Not all lenders will give second mortgages, while others only do so for people who have their first mortgages with them. The mortgage deals on offer are not always very competitive and different lenders can also have different attitudes.

Buying abroad inevitably introduces further risk, even if the lender has no direct interest in the foreign property. A poor purchase can mean pressure on finances elsewhere, which in turn can affect the ability to pay the mortgage. Not unreasonably, lenders are looking for as much security as possible. For example, Abbey National insists the person named on the mortgage is able to pay both the first and second home loans out of their own income, regardless of whether a partner will be contributing. Epsom-based National Counties Building Society will lend up to 70 per cent of a property's value and will want to check out borrower's income and payment records. Cheltenham & Gloucester will only let customers take a remortgage to buy a second home, but it will lend up to 95 per cent of a home's value.

WHICH TYPE OF MORTGAGE?

Whichever of the two routes borrowers go down, they do not need to be tied to their lender's floating standard variable mortgage rates. Borrowers can take out a fixed rate loan – fixing their payments to a set rate of interest for a set number of years. Alternatively, they can have a percentage knocked off the standard floating rate for some years.

Homeowners will usually have to stay with the borrower for a set number of years or pay an early redemption penalty for moving to a new lender. These penalties can be steep, and average out at six months' gross interest or 5 per cent of the loan.

Fixing gives certainty, but borrowers lose out if mortgage rates fall below the level of their fixed rates. The danger with discounted variable rates is that as interest rates rise, payments are dragged up, albeit it at a set percentage below the normal variable mortgage rate. But when mortgage rates fall, discounted mortgage holders do well as their payments drop. Mortgage tax relief is only available on a borrower's 'principal residence'. This basically means where you usually live. So if a borrower lives in a different home, be it in the UK or abroad, they lose this tax perk, which is now worth 10 per cent on the first £30,000 of the mortgage.

ARRANGING AN OVERSEAS LOAN TO BUY YOUR HOME

It is possible to obtain foreign currency mortgages where

homeowners take out a loan in the foreign country's currency, but pay it from a sterling bank account. Borrowers should avoid these home loans: they are a recipe for financial hardship. When the pound is strong against other currencies it looks tempting to use sterling's strength to buy a home in a different currency as it will buy much more. But this a very short-term and unwise view to take as the mortgage will be for perhaps 25 years and the fortunes of sterling versus the currency you are buying in will ebb and flow many times over this period.

As thousands of Britons discovered in the late 1980s, this is a very dangerous game to play. The values of currencies fluctuate against each other and borrowers who have to exchange their pounds for a foreign currency to pay their loan will find they have to dig ever deeper into their pockets when, as it inevitably will, the pound is no longer strong against the foreign currency. The simple message is – always borrow in the currency you earn in if at all possible.

This is particularly important as entry into European Monetary Union in 1999 has been ruled out. Had the UK committed itself to joining, then currencies such as sterling, the French franc and the Deutschmark would not fluctuate against each other as much as they do now. For the foreseeable future, sterling will bob up and down relative to other currencies.

Interest rates can move sharply over very short periods of time and this can cause a deal of hardship. Table 4.1 shows how the pound sterling has fared since January 1995 against the currencies of countries attracting many UK expatriates. As it shows, the fortunes of the pound go up and down.

Table 4.1 Movement of exchange rates against sterling,
January 1995–July 1997

Currencies	Jan 95	July 95	Jan 96	July 96	Jan 97	July 97
Deutschmark	2.362	2.145	2.185	2.303	2.574	2.836
French franc	8.12	7.48	7.47	7.76	8.65	9.53
Portugese escudo	242	225	225	235	257	284
Spanish peseta	200	187	183.45	192.7	215.94	238.29
Italian lire	2,478	2,533	2,348	2,322	2,536	2,763
US dollar	1.526	1.557	1.47	1.517	1.669	1.628
Australian dollar	1.95	2.19	1.95	1.91	2.08	2.14
New Zealand dollar	2.35	2.31	2.17	2.19	2.33	2.36
South African rand	5.20	5.59	5.34	6.54	7.68	7.26

(*Source*: Thomas Cook)

FOREIGN MORTGAGES

Britons abroad can get mortgages from lenders in the country they are living in. However, they may find that they need qualifications such as having been resident for a set number of years or be vouched for by their employers.

Similarly, the way mortgages are granted may be different. For example, the amount that can be borrowed may not depend on up to three or three and a half joint incomes as in the UK, but up to a set percentage of monthly income. The term of your mortgage may well be different and the amount you can borrow compared to the value of the property – called the loan-to-value – may also be different, and in many cases far lower than the usual 95 per cent in the UK; this means you need a deposit of as little as 5 per cent of the value of the home to get a mortgage.

Some countries also have odd little quirks. Malta, for example, says foreign nationals can borrow only up to 25 per cent of the value of a property, so you will need a pretty big deposit if you want a mortgage there.

As ever, the golden rule is to always borrow in the currency you are paid in if at all possible. Whether you are paid in sterling or that country's currency, you can usually get a mortgage from a lender there in the currency you want. The only major exceptions are France and the USA that insist in lending only in French francs and US dollars, respectively.

Mortgages are essentially the same wherever you are. You take out a loan for the value of all or part of your home and arrange to pay it back after a set period of time. You can either pay it off over the life of the loan – a repayment mortgage – or simply pay the interest and save up elsewhere to pay it off using those savings at a set date.

The most common way of saving to pay off a mortgage has always been with an endowment plan, a savings plan combining life insurance, using the cash lump sum paid from a pension or with a Personal Equity Plan (PEP). New government proposals mean that PEPs may no longer be suitable. As with UK mortgages, it is possible to have part of your home loan earmarked for home improvements. But this will usually have to be within the normal mortgage limits. Within this broad framework, different countries have different mortgage criteria.

Spain

You can take out a repayment or interest-only mortgage and pay it off with a PEP, endowment or pension. Usually you can borrow only up to 75 per cent of the property's value, although this can be increased to 80 per cent in some cases.

The smallest loan you can take out is £10,000, there is no maximum, and the term is 5 to 20 years. At the end of 1997 the mortgage interest rate was 1.5 per cent over LIBOR, a special interest rate used by banks trading money.

Portugal

Once again PEPs, endowments, pensions and repayments are acceptable. The most you can borrow is 75 per cent of the property's value. The term of the loan can be between 5 and 20 years and the minimum amount is £15,001. The interest rate is 1 per cent above LIBOR.

France

If you are buying a home in France you will very probably have to buy in French francs, which adds risk in the form of currency fluctuations. You can borrow up to 80 per cent of the value of the home and the minimum loan on offer is

£10,000. The loan can be for between 5 and 20 years, and fixed rate French franc mortgages are available.

United States

You are limited to a repayment mortgage and you can only raise it in US dollars. You can borrow 80 per cent of the property value, with a minimum of the equivalent value of £20,000. At the end of 1997 fixed rates of about 8 per cent were avilable to non-US residents. The rate is about 1 per cent lower for US citizens.

British lenders abroad

Major home loan firms such as the Woolwich (in France and Italy) and the Abbey National (in France, Italy and Spain), through subsidiaries Abbey National France and Abbey National Bank in Spain and Italy, also offer overseas mortgages through their overseas subsidiaries. But what they will and will not lend on varies from company to company as much as it does from country to country.

In addition, Gibraltar-based Abbey National Offshore will lend on properties in both Spain and Portugal, although it cannot lend to expatriates with Spanish residence permits or Spanish, Portugese or Gibraltarian nationals.

It will lend on all types of residential property provided it is structurally sound, is owned on a freehold basis or the lease has at least 30 years left to go and there are no third party charges on it. Loans of up to £400,000 are available with a minimum deposit of 35 per cent of the property's value and it will lend on two and a half times joint income less any outstanding liabilities or two and a half times the main income and one times the second – again, less any outstanding liabilities.

All Abbey National Offshore loans are made in sterling and the interest rate you pay is linked to the lending rates of three or four of the main UK banks. You can have either repayment or endowment mortgages.

The Woolwich will lend on properties in France through Banque Woolwich or Italy with Banca Woolwich. The mortgages you can get in each country are different. Its Italian mortgages must be paid in Italian lire and the most customers can borrow is 75 per cent of the value of the property. The longest term you can have a mortgage set up in Italy for is 30 years. How much you can borrow is not linked to income multiples. Instead, it is based on monthly payments up to a maximum of 35 per cent of gross monthly salary or salaries. The interest rate is linked to the Italian ABI Prime rate.

The most Banque Woolwich will lend on a French property is either 70 per cent of the lower of the valuation or purchase price, with a minimum loan of FF200,000, or if it is in a rural area 60 per cent of the value with a minimum loan of FF300,000. It has to be in Franch francs.

French law limits the maximum you can borrow to 33 per cent of gross monthly salary and Banque Woolwich insists on a minimum salary for a single applicant of FF140,000 (£14,736), or FF200,000 (£21,052) for joint applicants and in some rural areas, whether joint or single applicants, FF250,000 (£26,315).

The mortgage has to be for between 5 and 20 years and the interest rate you pay will depend on how big a deposit you are able to put down. In addition, Banque Woolwich says you must open a French bank account with a direct debit mandate before you can get a loan.

5

TAX AND THE EXPATRIATE

GOING abroad gives you a chance to escape the widespread net of the taxman. For some people the chance to avoid tax quite legally is a compelling reason for going abroad in the first place. However, legitimate tax avoidance (as opposed to tax evasion which is illegal) is not as easy as it might sound; and the British taxman's reach can be surprisingly difficult to shake off.

How long this reach is varies on your exact circumstances when abroad; are you working for a short time, for example, and intend to return later? Are you retiring abroad and intend to live there permanently? Are you going to be abroad for six months or so only? Do have you assets and investments in the UK? The law regarding tax and residency is a hotchpotch built up over the years and defined more by case law than by what is written down in the statutes. Your residency position as it affects the UK taxman depends on three key issues:

■   Are you 'resident' in the UK?

■   Are you 'ordinarily resident' in the UK?

■   Where are you domiciled?

Each is an important issue, but of the three the most crucial is also the most straightforward – whether you count as a UK resident or not.

ARE YOU RESIDENT IN THE UK?

Residency itself is usually an easy question to resolve, based on common-sense principles aimed at judging whether you really live in the country or not. Inevitably, however, the line has to be drawn somewhere, and sometimes the result can be rough justice. This is how the taxman assesses your position. The general rule is that you will be non-resident for a given tax year if you:

■ are in the UK for less than 182 days in each tax year, and

■ spend less than an average of 90 days in the UK over 4 consecutive tax years.

If the taxman agrees that you are non-resident, then all your overseas earnings will not be hit by UK income tax – it's as simple as that. Remember that in this context, a tax year runs from April 6 to the following April 5 – it is not at all the same thing as a calendar year. However, these limits on your visits to Britain are strictly applied to prevent you having your cake and eating it.

Expatriates have to carefully time their visits to the UK to make sure that they do not exceed their allowance – remember that planes can be delayed and people can fall ill, so prolonging your visit may jeopardize your residency status, and with it, bring you back within the clutches of the Inland Revenue. Sometime expatriates suffer through no fault of their own: many expatriates were hit hard after they had to flee Kuwait in the wake of the Iraqi invasion as this destroyed their non-resident status. These earnings may, of course, land you with a tax bill in the country where you are living but this is a different matter which we will explore below.

If you are abroad for less than a complete tax year, therefore, these rules will mean that you face UK income tax on your earnings. However, the Revenue is not entirely inhuman, and realizes that the demands of work do not neatly dovetail with the Revenue's definition of a tax year. So the taxman has devised something called the foreign earnings deduction. If you are working abroad for at least 365 days, which straddle two different tax years, you may be able to claim 100 per cent of your overseas earnings against tax.

The effect of this is that you will still avoid UK income tax if a year abroad does not precisely coincide with a tax year. However, this rule does not apply to Crown Servants, who are normally liable to UK income tax on overseas duties.

To qualify for this deduction, you do not have to remain out of the UK for the entire Qualifying period – but the rules which apply are slightly different. To get the foreign earnings deduction, you have to meet two qualifications:

■ make sure that no single visit is for more than 62 consecutive days, and

■ your total time in Britain must not be, at any time during the Qualifying period, more than one-sixth of the Qualifying period so far.

The difficulty of this rule, unfortunately, is that you have to plan whether any given break in the time abroad will still count to keep you below the one-sixth rule.

Example

Suppose:

■ you worked abroad for 30 days

■ returned to Britain for 10 days

■ and then worked abroad for 19 days.

This is a total of 59 days. Ten days is more than one-sixth of 59 days, and so these days cannot count towards the qualifying period needed to claim the

---

deduction. But if on the second occasion, you had worked abroad for 20 days instead of 19, the whole period would be then 60 days. As a result, the 10 days spent back home would not be more than one-sixth of the total and so all 60 days would count towards a qualifying period.

It is up to you to make sure that a UK employer sending you abroad for a period does not tax you under PAYE. This would be a disaster if you are being sent to a low tax country or even to one, such as Saudi Arabia, which does not levy personal income tax. If both you and your employer tell the tax office that is it likely that you will qualify for the foreign earnings deduction, it may be possible to have your salary paid gross under a 'no tax' code. You should write with full information about your stay abroad, and the tax office will then contact your boss to confirm the arrangements.

If the tax office does not have enough information to agree to this, you will be taxed under the PAYE system but will then be able to reclaim this when you fill in your tax return.

Days spent travelling to the UK do count as part of your 62-day allowance – but those travelling away from it do not. Leave pay following a qualifying period abroad is covered by the foreign earnings deduction. If you claim the foreign earnings deduction, you are still entitled to the normal personal allowance. You can use this to offset, for example, interest on investment income.

WHAT ABOUT ORDINARILY RESIDENT?

In the tax world 'ordinarily resident' is an irritatingly vague term which could almost be designed to lead to expensive legal disputes. Just like 'resident' itself, what it means is nowhere laid down in the Taxes Acts. One judge who was called upon to decide what it meant came up with the helpful definition that it means a person who was 'habitually and normally resident here apart from temporary or occasional absences'.

In practice, the Inland Revenue tend to wait for three years, and if you have been non-resident for those three years, will accept that you were – retrospectively – ordinarily non-resident for these years too. So what? Why does it matter?

Well, the concept of ordinary residence matters for Capital Gains Tax purposes. Someone who is not UK resident but is still ordinarily resident is still liable to UK capital gains tax on assets in the UK. This does not affect vast numbers of people – only around 70,000 are rich enough to get hit by gains above the annual exemption which was £6,500 for the 1997–98 tax year. But it can be a problem for people retiring to the sun and perhaps selling the family business, or hoping to realize gains beyond the taxman's reach. In this context, you may be able to benefit from something called an extra statutory concession, or ESC, which gives you a tax benefit to which you are not strictly entitled to in law.

One of these says that your date of being non-resident applies from the day after your departure, not, as could strictly speaking be the case, from the end of the tax year. By extension, your date of being regarded as not being ordinarily resident is also affected.

But it is not a good idea to realize enormous capital gains during the period between leaving the UK and the end of the tax year – ESCs are favours and not rights and are often put aside if the Revenue thinks you are deliberately exploiting them to avoid tax.

If you do realize a gain, and then revisit the UK in that tax year, the taxman could argue that in fact you were not even non-resident for that tax year.

Also, if you sell a business before going abroad, the date of the sale is the date of the contract – not the date you received the cash in a different country. Since the law of contract is complicated and subtle, and does not hinge upon the signing of a final legally binding contract, people can easily find that they made the contract before they left, and as such, are liable to a Capital Gains Tax (CGT) bill.

Remember, too, that the idea of being ordinarily resident implies a lengthy stay outside the UK. If you return within three years – for whatever reason – you will lose this, and will be liable for any CGT that you might otherwise have avoided.

SO HOW DO I ESTABLISH MY POSITION?

The answer is that the Inland Revenue will give you a ruling on this question if you ask. You need form P85 – Residence or Employment Abroad, available from any tax office. This is also used to allow you to claim any tax rebate you may be due for this tax year. If you are taxed under the PAYE system, for example, your salary throughout the year will be paid on the basis that your personal allowance will be spread evenly over 12 months. If you go abroad in month seven, for example, you will have therefore paid too much tax as you will only have been given seven-twelfths of your personal allowance.

Form P85 also asks for a lot of information about your future plans. When the taxman has assessed this, a provisional ruling on your residency status will be given. Oddly enough, there is no legal obligation on you to fill in this form or even tell the Inland Revenue that you are leaving Britain, but the sooner you do, the sooner you will be given a ruling on your status.

DOMICILE

The final concept which you will encounter if you plan to go abroad permanently – perhaps by retiring – is that of domicile. Domicile is a badly defined legal concept, but it basically refers to the country that you regard as your natural home, usually the place where you were born and lived in for most of your life. This matters because if you keep your English or Scottish domicile – remember, both countries have different legal systems – while living abroad, your heirs will be potentially liable to inheritance tax in the UK. This tax will be levied not just on assets within the UK, but on everything you own anywhere in the world.

From that point of view, it makes sense to shed your UK domicile if you are retiring abroad. However, this is not easy, and it is made worse by the fact that the Revenue will not give you a ruling on your domicile unless it becomes relevant for tax purposes, by which time you won't be around to argue the matter.

So it is up to you to provide your heirs with the evidence

they might need in the case of a dispute. When assessing your domicile, the taxman will look for evidence that you have permanently broken your connection with the UK. This might include:

- selling your home and assets in the UK

- buying property in your new country and acquiring financial assets there

- learning the language and becoming involved in the life of your new country

- making a will there – which you should do in any case

- taking out citizenship and renouncing that of the UK

- closing your UK bank account

- cancelling subscriptions to UK newspapers and magazines.

But is all this really worth it?

The Conservative Government tried hard to keep the inheritance tax down, and in the 1997–98 tax year the first £215,900 of your estate will escape inheritance tax. Inheritance tax planning is a very effective way of keeping the tax bill down. At the moment it is effectively a voluntary tax as any gifts made seven years before death are tax-free, and those made within seven years are subject to a tapering relief.

The days when you could shed UK residence status and not have to pay foreign tax are all but over, and so if you retire to Spain, for example, you will have to account to the *hacienda* – the Spanish tax gathering authority for your world-wide income. So shedding a UK domicile for a Spanish one may not save your heirs much in the way of tax.

This is a question upon which you need specialist advice. The answer depends on your personal circumstances, and the more assets you have accumulated during your life, the more important is such a decision. You need to find a good tax and financial adviser who can help you decide which is the best option.

FOREIGN TAXMEN

The days when British expatriates simply avoided foreign taxation are vanishing. While most Middle Eastern countries still levy no personal income tax, and some Far Eastern nations, such as Singapore, are lenient with expatriates, countries such as Spain, which were once lenient or inefficient are now neither. This partly reflects the streamlining and computerization of tax gathering, and means that even retirees living there can expect to be drawn into the tax net.

Tax residency is not at all the same thing as immigration status, and in most western European countries you are considered to be tax resident if you are in the country for 183 days or more during the year, and as in Britain, you may be liable for tax on your world-wide income. If this applies to you, it is your responsibility to contact the tax office. If you do not do so, you could easily be committing a criminal offence.

Do not try to escape being noticed – people leave huge paper trails these days, and tax offices have the power to subpoena important documents such as credit card bills. Modern technology means that a vast amount of information can be collated rapidly about you. You are also at risk of being denounced by someone you have offended, for whatever reason. Being illegal makes you vulnerable too; one London newspaper recently reported the case of some Britons in Spain who were dissatisfied with the huge charges their investment adviser was extorting for poor performance. He threatened to report them to the Spanish tax authorities if they didn't keep quiet.

You may find that you need a tax number to be allowed to open a bank account, which you will certainly need to do. Opening a bank account can be a tedious enough business at home, and is getting more difficult as identity checks tighten as part of the war against the drugs trade. It might be worth asking your bank at home for help – perhaps one of its correspondent banks in the country where you will be living can get things ready for you.

On the subject of banks, remember that the overdraft is a very British invention; in some countries, France in particular, it is a criminal offence to write a cheque if you do not have enough cash in your account to cover it. Persistent offenders are blacklisted throughout the country and have to survive with no bank account.

Problems with foreign taxmen can be exacerbated by the fact that the UK taxman will try to tax the income of people living abroad if it arises in the UK. This sounds innocuous, but in practice it means income from shares, unit trusts, building society accounts and property which is rented out can be taxed. This means that a lot of people are affected, because even people retiring to the sun are likely to keep a fair proportion of their assets in the UK, partly because they understand the language and traditions, and partly because they may not trust a foreign jurisdiction with their money. To make sure that you are not taxed twice on the same income – which could easily happen where you do not qualify for non-resident status in the UK, but the country where you are working does consider you a tax resident – the UK has signed double taxation treaties with most countries. Under these, each country agrees to give up or reduce its tax rights in certain circumstances. If there is no agreement in place, and you are still resident – in the UK, you can usually claim tax relief under UK tax law for foreign taxes which have been paid.

Working expatriates may be able to get tax relief immediately if your UK boss is required to deduct tax at source, and the foreign country insists that its taxes be deducted in the same way too. An easier solution is to try to keep some of your assets offshore, or in a jurisdiction such as the Channel Islands or the Isle of Man, where there is no local income tax, thus putting you beyond the reach of all taxmen.

THE TAXMAN'S LONG ARM

Many long-term expatriates retain assets in the UK – and these may fall within the taxman's reach, even if you are non-resident and not ordinarily resident either. This is the tax situation on various assets:

- Banks and building societies can pay you your interest free of tax if you sign a declaration that you are not UK resident. But money would still fall within the inheritance tax net even if you have a domicile outside of England or Scotland. Most expatriates use accounts in the Channel Islands or the Isle of Man which get round this disadvantage. They are also set up by branches of major UK institutions specifically for the expatriate market and so are geared up for your needs.

They usually pay higher rates of interest too (see Chapter 8).

■ Share-based investment, including unit trusts and investment trusts. Tax is deducted at source from dividends you get in the form of a tax credit voucher. As a general rule, it is not possible to claim this back if you are not a UK resident, although you can currently offset it against your UK personal tax allowance if you are a UK tax resident. You may be protected by a double taxation agreement, but it won't cover you for all your deduction, and in any case will involve you with the tax authorities in your new country. So unit trusts should be sold and replaced by offshore funds, which do the same thing but offshore.

■ Offshore funds are effectively unit trusts managed from offshore financial centres so that expatriates can escape the UK tax net.

■ Personal Equity Plans (PEPs) allow you to save up to £9,000 a year in shares or share-based investments and pay no tax. However, to qualify you have to be UK resident. When you go abroad, you may make no more contributions, but your existing PEP can stay in place. Do not shift this money offshore with you; if you do, when you return it cannot count as part of your PEP allowance for the preceding years, and as the future of PEPs is under government scrutiny, it is worth keeping these allowances.

■ Life insurance policies pay tax on the growth in the fund which is a disadvantage in investment terms. However, people who surrender early get hit hard by penalties, so keep these in place, and keep paying contributions even when abroad.

■ Gilts are securities issued by the UK government and, as such, the safest of all investments. Certain issues have no UK tax deducted if you are not ordinarily resident in the UK. A list can be obtained from the Bank of England (see Appendix). It is up to you to prove your status – if the Revenue has not yet accepted you as being not ordinarily resident, you will have to give evidence about your long-term intentions to be out of the country.

■ Property: if you let your UK home while you are abroad, you will have to pay tax on the income even if you have been classified as being not ordinarily resident. However, there is a lot you can deduct from this to reduce the bill (see Chapter 10 for full details).

6

PENSION PLANNING

WHETHER you are going abroad to retire in the sun, or to work there and intend to return to the UK later on, proper pension planning is vital. Anyone retiring abroad must go through a whole series of hoops to ensure that they get all of the pension they are entitled to, as well as ensuring the pension they do get does what they want it to. The Commonwealth is littered with pensioners living in straitened circumstances because they did not understand how their UK pensions work abroad before they went there.

Anyone intending to work abroad for any period of time must keep an eye on their pension. Not keeping up with both National Insurance contributions as well as paying into any company pension scheme that is available will mean a far lower income at retirement.

There are lots of different rules and regulations on who can do what with how much and when they can do it. Anyone considering living abroad either to work or for retirement should talk to the Department of Social Security, the Inland Revenue, their employer, their pension scheme and possibly an accountant specializing in advising people living outside the UK.

WORKING ABROAD

National Insurance

Paying National Insurance contributions while working abroad is not always compulsory, but it may be a very good idea to do so, if either you have little private pension provision set up, or you plan to return to the UK and rely on any of the State's welfare benefits.

There are two State pensions in the UK. The basic State pension, currently a maximum of £62.45 for the 1997–98 tax year, and the State Earnings Related Pension Scheme (SERPS), which is linked to how long you work and your earnings.

To get either of these pensions, National Insurance must be paid. In the case of the basic State pension, to get a full pension for yourself, or your widow, then you need a fairly full National Insurance record for your working life. The Department of Social Security defines someone's working life as from age 16 to one year before retirement age, which by the year 2010 will be 65 years old for men and women.

Similarly, getting as large a SERPS pension as possible means paying National Insurance. The SERPS pension is based on 20 years' worth of earnings so to get the most you can, you need to have paid National Insurance for this time.

Both these pensions will be paid to you regardless of whether you live in the UK or abroad when you retire. A whole host of other State benefits also rely on National Insurance contributions. These include incapacity benefit, the contributions-based jobseekers' allowance, maternity benefits as well as the State pension.

With so many benefits at stake, anyone who may return

There is a simple and legal way of reducing the amount of tax you will pay in the UK - simply move your UK savings to an offshore bank while you are living overseas.

To help you see if you could benefit from this, try answering the following questions:

1. Will you be overseas for a FULL UK TAX YEAR? **YES** ☐ **NO** ☐

2. Do you have SAVINGS IN THE UK? **YES** ☐ **NO** ☐

3. Do you have PROPERTY IN THE UK? **YES** ☐ **NO** ☐

4. Do you have any INVESTMENTS IN THE UK? **YES** ☐ **NO** ☐

If you ticked 'yes' to the first two questions and one other, there's a good chance you may have a tax liability you could legally reduce by banking offshore.

To find out more, contact Midland Offshore now, for a free copy of our brochure *'How to minimise your UK tax bill'* and details of the many benefits Midland Offshore can provide.

Midland Offshore
Member HSBC *Group*

Making your money work harder

☎ **Call 44 1534 616111**
24 hours a day

Fax 44 1534 616222
24 hours a day

✂ Or cut this coupon

To: Midland Offshore, PO Box 615, 28/34 Hill Street, St. Helier, Jersey JF4 5YD, Channel Islands.
Please send me my copy of "How to minimise your UK tax bill"

Name_____

Nationality _____

Address _____

_____

_____

_____Tel _____   MM/0198

to the UK during their working lives or once they have retired should think long and hard about paying National Insurance while they are abroad.

If you are employed by a company and earn, in tax year 1997–98, between £61.99 and £465 a week – what are called the Lower and Upper Earnings limits – you will have to pay Class 1 National Insurance contributions. Anyone going to work abroad has to keep on paying Class 1 contributions for the first 52 weeks they are away provided:

- your employer has a base in the UK

- you are an ordinary resident of the UK. Basically, you are if you normally live in the UK despite the odd absence and you have a settled mode of life there

- you were resident in the UK immediately before you went abroad to work.

The rates of National Insurance paid are exactly the same as you would pay if you still lived in the UK and your employer will pay them for you. If you do not pay Class 1 contributions for the first 52 weeks, you cannot later pay either Class 2 contributions, usually paid by the self-employed, or Class 3 voluntary contributions instead. The result will be a gap in your National Insurance record and this will restrict the benefits you can claim in the UK as well as cut the value of your eventual State pensions.

If you are not liable to pay Class 1 contributions, it is possible to pay Class 2 contributions voluntarily to stop a gap appearing. The employed and the self-employed can pay them if:

- you lived in the UK for a continuous three-year period at any time before you pay the contributions or you paid a set amount of contributions before you went abroad for three years

- you are working abroad but are not liable to pay Class 1 contributions and were employed or self-employed immediately before you went abroad

- you would normally be self-employed or employed, but were out of a job just before you went abroad.

It is also possible to pay voluntary Class 3 contributions to protect your pension. You can pay them if:

- you paid Class 1 contributions for your first year abroad.

- or you lived in the UK for a three-year stretch before going abroad or paid a set amount of National Insurance contributions for at least three years before you left.

Your employer will pay your Class 1 contributions for your first year abroad. Class 2 and 3 contributions can be paid either by direct debit, annually or by an agent you have nominated. To do this you will need form CF 83 from your local benefits office.

PAYING INTO PRIVATE PENSIONS

The rules over which types of UK pension schemes you can and cannot pay into are confused and seem to make no sense. You can pay into a company pension scheme set up by your employer in the UK, provided you are employed by a UK taxable company or it is subject to UK tax. But you cannot pay in to a personal pension plan. These were first made available in 1988 and are aimed at allowing people without access to a company pension scheme to build up a pension. These personal pensions only accept earnings from employment in the UK.

Similarly, you cannot pay in to an old-style 226 or retirement annuity contract, the precursor to personal pensions, if you are working abroad. The great advantage of UK pensions is that both the money you and your employer pay in and the investment growth while it is invested are largely free of tax. While the UK's Inland Revenue is perfectly happy for your money to grow tax-free, the tax authorities in the country you live in may not be so generous. So it is vital to talk to your company pension scheme manager as some countries may try to tax the employer's contributions as a benefit in kind.

In the worst possible scenario, the taxman in a foreign country may decide that not only are employer's contributions benefits in kind, but the money in the fund is too, so they may try to tax the investments. There have been cases in the USA where this has been tried.

RECEIVING YOUR PENSION ABROAD

All types of pensions that have been built up over your working life can be paid directly to you if you decide to live overseas once you have retired. This applies to basic State pensions, SERPS pensions as well as company and all types of individual pensions.

If you are already abroad, the Department of Social Security will get in touch with you four months before retirement age if it still has your address. The basic State

Further Kogan Page titles...

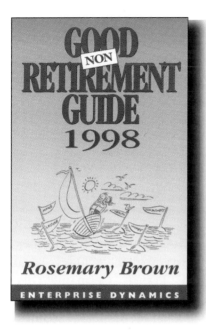

"...packed with advice to make retirement financially sound - and fun."
SUNDAY EXPRESS

"a mine of useful information...well worth the purchase price."
THE INDEPENDENT

"If you are within five years of retirement or have retired already, this guide is compulsory reading."
GLASGOW HERALD

"The author has done for the management of personal affairs at the end of the century what Mrs Beeton did for households at the end of the last. Excellent"
CA JOURNAL

People are often unsure how best to plan for their future - a future without work. The increased amount of leisure time, financial, home and health concerns are all important considerations during retirement. This book explains how to make the most of every minute of the retiree's time and money.

CONTENTS

Introduction • Looking Forward to Retirement • Money in General • Pensions • Tax • Investment • Financial Advisors • Budget Planner • Your Home • Leisure Activities • Starting Your Own Business • Looking for Paid Work • Voluntary Work • Health • Holidays • Caring for Elderly Parents • No one is Immortal • Index

£14.99 • 12th Edition • Paperback • 512 pages • ISBN 0 7494 2551 2

To order please contact our Customer Services Department at:
Kogan Page Ltd. 120 Pentonville Road, London, N1 9JN.
Tel 0171 278 0545 Fax. 0171 278 8198

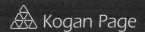

pension will be paid to you no matter where you are. But depending where you live, once you leave the UK you may lose your entitlement to its annual increases, which are usually in line with prices. This causes great distress to a large number of people who have retired mainly to Commonwealth countries. A government inquiry in 1997 investigated whether annual increases should be paid, but a cross-party committee of MPs voted not to.

COUNTRIES WHERE YOUR UK BASIC STATE PENSION WILL NOT RISE IN LINE WITH PRICES INCLUDE: Australia, New Zealand, South Africa and Canada.

COUNTRIES WHERE YOUR UK BASIC STATE PENSION WILL BE REGULARLY INCREASED ARE: all countries in the European Economic Area which includes Austria, Belgium, Denmark, Finland, France, Germany, Greece, Iceland, Italy, Liechtenstein, Luxembourg, the Netherlands, Norway, Portugal, the Republic of Ireland, Spain and Sweden, as well as the UK including Gibraltar.

There are also agreements with a number of other countries, so pensioners will get their annual increases there too. These countries are: Barbados, Bermuda, Bosnia-Herzegovina, Croatia, Cyprus, Republic of Macedonia, Guernsey, Mauritius, Philippines, Israel, Jamaica, Jersey, Malta, Sark, Switzerland, Slovenia, Turkey and the USA.

Your SERPS pension will always get the annual increases that anyone living in Great Britain gets. There is no discrimination against pensioners deciding to live in any particular country.

Retirement income from company pension schemes and all types of individual pensions such as personal pensions can be paid to you regardless of where you live. In the same way, you will always get any annual increases that someone

with the same pension in the UK would get. The pension is also subject to UK tax.

Pensions from UK schemes are usually paid in sterling. If you live abroad, it may be possible to pay the pension directly to you, rather than into a bank account in the UK. It may also be possible to have that pension paid in the currency of the country you live in, rather than sterling. It will still be subject to UK tax.

It is possible to take the money you have built up in your pension scheme and buy an income or annuity from a life insurance company in another European Union country. This would mean the income is paid in that country's currency, but taxed from the UK. The company must be authorized in the European Union. In practice, buying an annuity like this is very rare indeed.

DOUBLE TAXATION AGREEMENTS

If you are permanently resident overseas it is possible to have your pension income from the UK paid to you without being hit by UK tax. Instead, you will pay the normal tax that other people in the country you live in pay. Whether or not this is a good idea will depend on the tax rates in the country you live in. If it is lower, you win, if it is higher, you lose. If you return to live in Great Britain, you will have to revert to paying UK tax again.

There are also what are called double taxation agreements between the UK and other countries. These agreements mean you will not be taxed any higher than the tax rate of the country you are living in. For example, if your pension is subject to 20 per cent tax in the UK, but the tax

182ml

rate in the country you live in is 30 per cent, then you just pay an extra 10 per cent in the other country.

Nearly 100 countries have struck double taxation agreements with the UK. They are: Antigua and Bermuda, Australia, Austria, Azerbaijan, Bangladesh, Barbados, Belarus, Belgium, Belize, Bolivia, Botswana, Brunei, Bulgaria, Canada, China, Croatia, Cyprus, Czech Republic, Denmark, Egypt, Estonia, Falkland Islands, Faroe Islands, Fiji, Finland, France, Gambia, Germany, Ghana, Greece, Grenada, Guernsey, Guyana, Hungary, Iceland, India, Indonesia, Republic of Ireland, Isle of Man, Israel, Italy, Ivory Coast, Jamaica, Japan, Jersey, Kenya, Kiribati, Republic of Korea, Lesotho, Luxembourg, Macedonia, Malawi, Malaysia, Malta, Mauritius, Mexico, Monserrat, Morocco, Myanmar (formerly Burma), Namibia, Netherlands, New Zealand, Nigeria, Norway, Pakistan, Papua New Guinea, Philippines, Poland, Portugal, Romania, Russian Federation, St Kitts and Nevis, Sierra Leone, Singapore, Slovak Republic, Slovenia, Solomon Islands, South Africa, Spain, Sri Lanka, Sudan, Swaziland, Sweden, Switzerland, Thailand, Trinidad and Tobago, Tunisia, Turkey, Tuvalu, Uganda, Ukraine, USA, Uzbekistan, Vietnam, Yugoslavia, Zambia and Zimbabwe.

The worst thing that can happen is to be in a country without a double taxation agreement. You may then find yourself in the appalling position of having to pay a full amount of UK tax and then the full tax rate from your host country on top of that.

OTHER OPTIONS

Wherever you retire, if your income is paid from a UK pension scheme, then it will have to be converted into another currency. Inevitably this means you will be at the mercy of currency fluctuations. When sterling is strong, you will do well, but when it is weak, the value of your pension where you live will fall.

One way around this is to buy an annuity from a European Union authorized insurer in the country you live in. This rarely happens and although it may solve one problem, you may find you do not get such a good deal from the annuity itself as you would from a UK one.

The other solution is to transfer your entire pension to another country. This is very, very risky and, again, is extremely rare. Not all countries are as generous with their tax on pension schemes as the UK is.

Tax relief is a big factor in helping UK pensioners get as big an income as possible. Other countries may not give so much tax relief. They may also restrict what pension funds in that country you can invest in. UK fund managers are famous for delivering good returns by investing in company shares. Other countries may simply not have the fund managers with sufficient expertise to match what you could have got in the UK.

7

INVESTMENTS FOR EXPATRIATES

GOING abroad is a great chance to accumulate some capital tax-free. For some people it's the only chance they will ever have and so it has to be made the most of. But not surprisingly, making your money grow for you is easier said than done, even when your circumstances mean that the tax-man's dues do not have to feature so strongly in your calculations. The truth is that human nature seems to conspire to make us our own worst enemy when it comes to making our money work harder for us.

With that in mind, the first steps to financial freedom consist in thoroughly understanding some basic investment truths and building your investment strategy around them.

THE MORE RISK YOU TAKE – THE MORE YOU MAKE

There is a real trade-off between risk and reward. Those who opt for safety at all costs will never make a great deal of money. This is because the price of safety is putting everything into the bank or building society where interest rates move up and down, and are eroded in real terms by inflation.

If the interest is spent – to top up a pension, for example – then inflation eats into the real value of capital at an alarming rate. If you start out with £10,000, and inflation is 3 per cent for five years, then in real terms, your £10,000 has been reduced to £8,587 five years later, and £7,374 ten years later. With inflation at higher levels, the effect is more alarming still – at 5 per cent, £10,000 gets reduced to £7,737 after five years, and £5,987 after ten.

Over the long term, money put into the stock market is likely to make your money grow much more. For example, if you had invested £1,000 in the Halifax Solid Gold account, a 90 day investment account where your capital is totally safe, on 1 August 1987, it would have been worth £1,911 ten years later assuming that the interest was reinvested and allowed to grow instead of being spent. The same amount invested in the average UK unit trust would have grown to £2,329, assuming again that dividends had been reinvested. The difference is clear enough but in fact, the unit trust performance is more impressive than it sounds, for over that 10-year period, two factors distorted the statistics: the crash of 1987 reduced the value of your unit trust stake by around a fifth in a few days, and the building society figure was inflated by a period of unusually high interest rates which hit 15 per cent in the early 1990s.

Of course, it is quite true that this is a risk investment, and the stock market is subject to periodic booms and slumps, and a bad correction in the market can wipe away

"I *do* bank offshore I *don't* have instant access to my money do I need the International Debit Card from Standard Chartered or *don't I* ?"

If you keep money offshore, you may have all the confidence of knowing it is in a secure environment arning a competitive rate of interest. But what about getting your hands on it hen you need it? Your offshore bank is probably a long way away and, until ow, getting access to your money may have been a slow and cumbersome rocess.

THE INTERNATIONAL DEBIT CARD

Our International Debit Card can help to put your offshore money right into ur hands, giving you easy, instant access to it from around the world.

The Card bears the VISA symbol, allowing you to withdraw local currency m over 360,000 24-hour VISA cash machines around the globe and to make ect payments from your offshore bank account for goods and services at over million outlets worldwide – wherever you see the VISA symbol.[*]

Available with our **Sterling, US Dollar and now with our Deutsche Mark counts,** the International Debit Card can help put your offshore funds right o your pocket.

For more information about our International Debit Card and the Sterling, Dollar and Deutsche Mark Accounts, please return the coupon which can be und at the end of this chapter to:

s Ruth Martin, Standard Chartered Bank (CI) Limited, Box 830, Conway Street, St Helier, Jersey JE4 0UF, annel Islands. Or call us on Jersey +44 (0) 1534 507001. : +44 (0) 1534 507112.

of the Card is subject to the conditions described in the applicable International Debit Card Terms and Conditions.
International Debit Card is available to Extra Value Deposit Account Customers who hold a minimum of £2,500 or US$5,000 heir account with the Jersey Office of Standard Chartered Bank (CI) Limited.

rincipal place of business of Standard Chartered Bank (CI) Limited is Jersey, and its paid-up capital and reserves exceed £39 million. es of the latest audited accounts are available on request.

sits made with the office of Standard Chartered Bank (CI) Limited in Jersey are not covered by the Deposit Protection me under the UK Banking Act 1987. Jersey is not part of the UK.

Standard ⚡ Chartered

part of your capital. There are ways of minimizing the risk which will be considered shortly, but the essential fact remains: the more risk you can take on board, the better your chances of making your money grow.

SO HOW MUCH RISK CAN YOU HANDLE?

This is really a question about you. What is your personal risk profile? How strong are your nerves? If you will worry every time there is a bad spell on the stock market, you need to think hard about whether shares are really for you. Even although you are overwhelmingly more likely to make more money from buying shares than by leaving it in the bank, the accompanying anxiety and stress might not make it worthwhile.

Even so, however, the risk of the stock markets is dramatically reduced if you can plan ahead. The real danger of the stock market is concentrated into very short periods of time. If you can think long term, and not worry too much about this, your money is still likely to grow, despite short-term slumps. Those who get badly hurt in stock market crashes are the people who need to sell shares at a time when prices are depressed. Take comfort from the fact that shares in well-run companies tend to increase their dividends at a rate faster than inflation, and this tends to drive the share price upwards over time along with it.

Of course, the wise investor will not have everything in the stock market – you should always have enough money in the building society, either in an instant access account or at say 30 days' notice so you can get at it quickly in case of emergency.

REDUCING THE RISK

Regular savings

For all but the most active and resolute of investors, who have the time and inclination to watch the markets on a daily basis, regular savings provide the answer. If you put regular amounts into the stock market each month, you do not need to worry about getting the timing right. It averages out your buying costs too, as your stake buys fewer shares when prices are high, and rather more when they are low. Better still, you do not notice the money you are investing, your monthly budget adjusts to cover the gap, and so regular saving becomes a painless way of building up capital.

Regular savings is also a good idea for the nervous investor, who would otherwise have sleepless nights on reading of a bad day on the stock market.

Diversifying your investments

Holding your money in the shares of just a few companies is a high risk strategy – what would happen if one of them were to go bust? Instead, invest through an offshore fund, very similar to the familiar UK unit trusts, where your money is pooled with that of thousands of other small investors and then used to buy shares in hundreds of different companies – they won't all go bust at once.

Stock market guaranteed funds

There is a much wider choice of investment vehicles today,

Offshore banking with no hang-ups

When you're a long way from your offshore bank it's reassuring to know you can phone in and sort out your payments, arrange standing orders and check on your balance seven days a week - even out of normal banking hours.

Our telephone banking service for Overseas Club Members is set up to provide just such a service with sophisticated security arrangements and well-trained staff.

However, most expatriates need more than this.

You need information on mortgages, international money transfers, property management, insurance and pensions.

You may need help on choosing suitable savings or investment plans.

You may need information on choosing a UK school and help in providing the funds for it.

For this you need to know you can speak personally to your contacts in the bank and be confident that they understand your special circumstances. That's why Lloyds Bank set up the Overseas Club account back in the 1980s. As a result, we have enormous experience in dealing with the expatriate's total banking requirements. Today tens of thousands of expatriates rely on Lloyds Bank and the Overseas Club.

Benefits include:

- A personal Club Executive and supporting team
- Premium interest paid gross
- The choice of sterling or dollars* as the currency for the account
- Credit and debit cards
- Cheque book facility on sterling account
- A regular magazine which includes details of new products; tax matters; countries of special interest to expatriates as well as other Members' experiences
- Special discounts on a range of different items such as removals and language courses
- Introductions to our investment managers
- Help with retirement planning

Club Members can also meet managers from our Offshore Centres on their frequent visits to countries around the world. There they can discuss personal financial requirements and any worries they may have.

The Lloyds Bank Overseas Club truly offers a one-stop offshore banking service with no hang-ups.

Call our information line on:

+44 (0) 990 258 079

Lloyds Bank

...NGING THE PERSONAL TOUCH TO OFFSHORE BANKING

...oyds Bank Offshore Centre,
...Box 12, Douglas, Isle of Man,
...tish Isles IM99 1SS.
...x +44 (0) 1624 638 181
...p://www.lloyds-offshore-bank.com.
...tres also in Jersey and Guernsey.

Please send to: Lloyds Bank Offshore Centre, PO Box 12, Douglas, Isle of Man, British Isles IM99 1SS for a brochure on the Lloyds Bank Overseas Club and details of the Offshore Centres.

Title_____ Last name_____

First names_____

Address_____

_____

Phone number (daytime)_____

MM 1/98

and by using modern investment techniques such as derivatives and options, fund managers have been able to lauch a range of investments that enable you to lock in some, if not all, of the gains from your investment.

INCOME VERSUS CAPITAL

Naturally, how you approach finance will depend a great deal on your own position. Someone working in the Gulf for three years will have very different needs and aspirations than someone retiring to Spain's Costa del Sol after a lifetime of work.

For the short-term expatriate, the main opportunity on offer is the chance to accumulate capital quickly, often in a country where you are paying no UK or local taxes on your income, and have very little to spend your salary on either. For such a person, the stock market has to be the main priority. It is the place to make your money grow over the longer term and substantial investment now will pay dividends later.

The other financial priority, however, might be to reduce your level of debt. This means, particularly, a mortgage on your UK home. With mortgage rates at around the 7–9 per cent level, this works out as quite expensive with inflation at such low rates. Using part of your money to get this debt down makes sound financial sense, as well as giving you a warm glow inside.

Some loans come with penalties if you repay them within a specified period, but if they do not, consider repaying debt a top priority. However, a retired person has a different priority. The main need is for income to top up a pension. It

does not make sense to take huge risks with capital as it is this capital which is providing the extra income.

But there is a trap waiting here for the unwary. It is very tempting to go for the highest possible income today, completely disregarding the fact, which many investors do not fully realize, that there is a trade-off in investment terms between high income and high capital growth.

Some investments are designed first of all to pay an income. This is true obviously of building societies and banks, but it true to a certain extent of some investment funds, which buy the shares of firms paying above average dividends to their shareholders.

Funds at the other end of the capital v income spectrum aim to identify shares in fast-growing companies which pay low dividends today, preferring instead to plough the money back into the business to make it grow. Each are designed to satisfy the needs of different people, which are sometimes decided by tax considerations, sometimes by age.

But the rule to remember is that an investment which will give you an above average income today can only do so at the risk of giving you less potential to make your money grow in the longer term. In extreme cases, some investments paying a very high income may be paying it out of your capital. You may be happy to accept this and, after all, an investment which hopes to provide your reward by making your money grow in the medium term may fail to do so.

But consider this. Since life expectancy is growing rapidly, and people can now expect to survive into their eighties, it is absolutely essential to put money into an investment which will give you the chance of increasing your income as the years go by.

Remember how quickly inflation can erode the real value

of your capital if it is left in the building society and the income is spent. It probably makes sense to settle for a little less income today in the hope of seeing it keep pace with – or better – beating inflation in the longer term. Many Britons who had retired to Spain learned this the hard way in the early 1990s, when interest rates were over 12 per cent. Many held all their assets in Gibraltar banks, getting tax-free income, only to get caught by a triple blow:

■ interest rates eventually fell, reducing their income

■ inflation eroded the value of their capital as all the interest was being spent to support the lifestyle, and

■ the Spanish peseta increased in value against the pound, so reducing the buying power of the interest still further.

For many people, the result was serious financial hardship.

KEEPING HOLD OF YOUR MONEY

Making money is a difficult enough business without having to think how you will keep hold of it. In the UK, a raft of investor protection law exists to protect your money in cases of fraud. Some of it was introduced as part of the Financial Services Act, which was itself born out of the need to curb scandalous practices in the investment business. Some, but not all offshore investments, are similarly protected.

Banks

The Deposit Protection Scheme gives you compensation of up to 90 per cent of your cash, up to a maximum of £20,000 in cases of insolvency by a UK bank. But it does not cover their offshore subsidiaries. The Isle of Man compensation scheme covers up to 75 per cent of the first £20,000 deposited, and the protection extends to non-sterling deposits. Really nervous investors may prefer to have several different accounts below the threshold to obtain maximum protection. Surprisingly, Jersey and Guernsey do not have similar legislation in place, preferring to limit bank licences to reputable names only.

Building societies

Again, you are covered for up to 90 per cent up to £20,000 in case of insolvency. In practice, building societies are a very safe investment and in cases of failure, the society has simply been taken over by a stronger rival. Under UK law, building societies must protect investments of their offshore subsidiaries.

Investment funds

In the UK you are protected in the case of insolvency or fraud by the Investors Compensation Scheme with unit trusts having to be authorized by the trade and industry department. Offshore, the situation varies. The Guernsey authorities must be satisfied with the probity of all parties involved in the running of the fund. In Luxembourg, the assets of the fund, which represent your money, must be held by a custodian, which is usually a bank, but which cannot be the same company as the fund manager. This protects you if the fund manager fails.

Four places have been given designated territory status by the UK government. To get this, their regulation and supervision have to be of a UK standard, and this includes a compensation scheme to protect investors in the case of fraud. The four are the Isle of Man, Guernsey, Jersey, and Bermuda.

Under the Guernsey scheme, you are protected for 90 per cent of the first £50,000, and then 30 per cent of the balance up to £100,000, making a total of £48,000. In Jersey, compensation covers you for 100 per cent of the first £30,000, and then 90 per cent of the balance up to £50,000 making a maximum of £48,000. In the Isle of Man the compensation limit for investment funds is 100 per cent of the first £30,000 and then 90 per cent of next £20,000, to a maximum of £48,000.

Life insurance

The Policyholders Protection Act, which provides consumers with up to 90 per cent of policy benefits in case of failure, only covers insurers registered in the UK. Offshore, you depend entirely on the legislation operating where the insurer is actually based.

In the UK, the financial advisory business is strictly regulated. Anyone selling anything financial to you has to give what is known as 'best advice'. This means the best advice for your circumstances and, in particular, means that the adviser must not give you the advice which gives him or her the most commission.

Offshore, as you would expect, you cannot expect to be protected to this degree. The general rule, although it is

hedged about with qualifications, is that a UK salesman offshore need not necessarily have to provide UK levels of disclosure.

If you buy from someone outside the UK regulatory network, you will get exactly the degree of protection afforded you by the laws where the adviser is regulated. In the worst case scenario, this could mean none at all.

It makes sense to follow a strict safety first rule in your investment strategy when you are sailing in offshore waters. In many jurisdictions, offshore, pretty much anything goes. Many places have set themselves up as offshore financial centres to boost flagging economies. All such places are concerned about is providing business for local solicitors and accountants and getting contributions to tax revenue. They will not be too bothered if you get ripped off by a company based and registered there, and you will have no comeback if it does. There will be no Ombudsman scheme, and no compensation scheme either.

There are two rules of self-protection which you should always follow:

- Only put your money with subsidiaries of household-name companies in the financial world back home. That way, you benefit from the financial strength and reputation of the UK company, which would not allow its name to be hit by an offshore scandal. Avoid companies you have never heard of.

- Look for investments from companies based in one of the more reputable offshore centres, where some protection rules have been set up and where banks, insurance companies and investment houses are properly regulated. This means, in practice, the Isle of Man, the

Channel Islands and Bermuda. It is not worth trying to squeeze the last penny from your investments if it means taking a risk with money by backing an unknown firm based in an obscure corner of the world.

DANGER – ROGUES!

Expatriates are a prime target for rogues and conmen who find life much more difficult in the UK where financial regulation is tougher. Offshore, people have a lot of money to invest and need to find somewhere to invest it. Yet this need to accumulate capital quickly, or to top up a pension, makes people oddly vulnerable to a variety of get-rich-quick-schemes which usually end up making you much poorer. As an expatriate, you are a honey-pot of cash; you won't need to seek out profitable investment opportunities – they seek you out.

The general rule – the golden rule, in fact – is that if an investment proposition seems too good to be true, that's because it is. There are no exceptions to this rule. No investment can deliver high income today and soaring capital growth potential – it's a circle which cannot be squared and those who say otherwise are liars.

Any investment scheme which offers you the chance of a well above average return has to be taking above average risks to provide it. And that's assuming any such scheme is on the level anyway. More often, the lure of huge returns is designed to part you from your hard-earned money. Bear these facts in mind constantly and you should be all right. Don't be greedy about money, be content to let it grow slowly.

The tell-tale signs of a fraud include the following: too-clever-by-half schemes which you don't fully understand, complicated tax evasion strategies which are unnecessary when you can avoid most tax offshore perfectly legitimately, schemes where you have to buy now with no time to reflect and study what is on offer, and schemes which are so good that you are told not to discuss them with anyone else.

Beware of, in particular:

- investment in commodities such as grain, or heavy metals, and futures, where heavy charges and rapid price changes can decimate your capital. Margin trading means that, eg, a 10 per cent price change can wipe you out and this may not be made clear to you.

- so-called alternative investments, such as diamonds, sapphires, precious metals, scotch whisky, or rare stamps. The sting is that the value you buy at is hugely inflated and the market in which you sell is restricted or even non-existent. Some of these commodities are not as rare as common sense might dictate. There is no shortage of industrial diamonds, for example.

- pyramid-type schemes, where the source for your return comes from subscriptions paid by newcomers to the scheme, although the promoters will try hard to disguise this fact. These eventually collapse when there are no more recruits, those last in lose their entire stake, and the real money goes to the promoters.

- investment in worthless shares. They are not described as such, of course, but there have been a number of telephone-based hustlers urging you to buy shares in tiny companies, often quoted on the NASDAQ market in the USA, or on the Vancouver or Alberta stock exchanges in Canada. Unscrupulous promoters buy up huge blocks of shares in shell companies and push them onto investors through high pressure selling techniques at hugely inflated prices. Buyers who want to sell soon find this is impossible as no market exists, or is only possible at a large loss. Shares in mining, high-technology and biotechnology companies are especial favourites for this kind of scam because few people understand the issues, and those who do not will rarely admit it.

8

SAVINGS AND INVESTMENT GUIDE

BANK AND BUILDING SOCIETY ACCOUNTS

BANKS and building society accounts are essential for everyone as a place to park money you do not immediately need when you are living abroad. With banks, choose a subsidiary of one of the big names from the UK. It is best to use offshore accounts in the Channel Islands or the Isle of Man. They are geared up to the special needs of people living and working abroad, and they often pay higher returns than their UK equivalents. This is because they do not have to share in the costs of the UK branch network. Expatriates living in southern Spain often prefer to use banks across the border in Gibraltar for the convenience of access, but again, choose a subsidiary of a big financial name. No tax is deducted from your interest.

Do not have money you do not need straightaway lying around in instant access accounts as you can get higher interest by agreeing to give notice to get at your cash. Some of the best returns go to so-called High Interest Cheque

first thought

Get wise.

The Abbey National range of Offshore Deposit Accounts is designed to meet the needs of the international investor, offering high flying interest rates in three currencies.

As an Abbey National Offshore investor, your money is safe and secure in Jersey, one of the world's most successful finance centres. What's more, it's guaranteed by Abbey National plc. And it's easy to get at, so if you have to make a sudden swoop, you needn't worry - your money is there for you.

Get wise as to how Abbey National in Jersey can help your money to grow. Complete and post or fax the coupon today for details and a copy of our informative booklet.

We currently offer a choice of five Savings Accounts:

OFFSHORE INSTANT
Sterling - *gives you immediate access to your money with six tiers of interest rates.*

OFFSHORE 90
Sterling - *subject to 90 days' notice but offers you a higher rate of interest.*

OFFSHORE 180
Sterling - *subject to 180 days' notice offering four tiers of even higher interest rates.*

OFFSHORE US DOLLAR CALL
with four tiers of interest rates.

OFFSHORE DEUTSCHEMARK CALL
with four tiers of interest rates.

Funds can be paid and received in most major currencies.

Abbey National, one of the world's strongest banking groups

The Abbey National group is rated AA by Standard & Poors

- ✂

Please send me full details of your Offshore Deposit Accounts along with your current interest rates and a copy of your free booklet, 'Offshore Investment with Abbey National'

To:

Julie O'Hanlon *Marketing Assistant*

Abbey National
   Treasury International Limited
PO Box 545, Jersey JE4 8XG
Channel Islands

Fax: +44 1534 885050

Name (Mr/Mrs/Miss/Ms)

Address

Telephone   Fax   MMD1

Money Mail Moves Abroad

HANSARD

Large enough to count...
...small enough to care

When you're ready to invest offshore you're ready for Hansard.

Hansard is exclusively an offshore company operating on the Isle of Man. With 27 currencies and over 100 funds to select from together with an extensive range of products designed to cover all your regular savings, lump sum, personalised portfolio and protection needs – there is probably no other offshore company that can offer you a wider choice.

Quite impressive don't you think?

But what's more impressive is our commitment to our broker network and investment in technology which enables us to provide a better standard of service – perhaps that's why in the last six years we've won over sixty awards for products, fund performance and service.

So when you're ready, ask your financial advisor about Hansard.

Hansard International Limited
PO Box 192, Anglo International House
Bank Hill, North Quay, Douglas
Isle of Man, IM99 1QL
Telephone +44 1624 688000
Facsimile +44 1624 688135
http://www.hansard.com
Registered No. 32648

H-1098-O 11/97

Accounts, where you get a cheque book which can be used for writing cheques, although with some accounts a minimum cheque level is set.

The risk of buying is concealed. Although apparently there is no risk, money left on deposit in this way will not grow by very much if you reinvest the interest, and if you spend it – to top up a pension, for example – it will be eroded by inflation. So do not put everything on deposit. This is a particular temptation when interest rates are very high. The problem is that rates spend as much time going down as they do going up! Check rates frequently too: today's top account may be a middle-of-the-road performer in a year's time.

OFFSHORE FUNDS

These are effectively the equivalent of the unit trusts found onshore, and many are offered by the same household-name investment companies. Like unit trusts, they pool your savings with those of thousands of other small investors, and so get you a spread of risk on the stock market which you couldn't achieve for yourself.

Like any stock market investment, you get a balance of income and capital growth. Some funds give you a choice as to whether your income is paid out (distributor funds) or reinvested for you to grow further (accumulator or roll-up funds).

For all this you are likely to pay an up-front entry fee of around 5 per cent of what you invest, plus between 1–1.5 per cent of the fund value each year. These charges vary between funds – the cost of running a bond or gilt fund is less than that of a fund looking for shares in underdeveloped markets,

Kids' Play?

Traditional Routes ... Global Expertise

Bank of Ireland Asset Management (BIAM) is the investment management arm of the Bank of Ireland Group. Since its foundation in 1966, it has been a major force in Irish fund management. From this solid foundation, and nurtured by the skills of its experienced investment team, BIAM has grown a truly global business, with a proven track record of consistent long-term performance.

An integral part of this success story has been the offshore funds managed by the BIAM group – in particular, Bank of Ireland Global Funds, launched by the group in 1983. Over the years, thousands of investors have made these funds their choice for long-term growth ... investors from places as far apart as Ireland and South Africa, the UK and Bermuda, Spain and Singapore. In addition to attracting investors the world over, the funds have established an enviable track record, scooping many investment awards over the years.

Best Small Offshore Fund Manager 1988-90

Micropal

Fixed Interest Fund Management Group of the Year – 1991 & 1994

Investment International

Best Mixed Fund Manager over 1 & 5 years

Portfolio International Offshore Fund Awards 1995

Best Offshore Fund Manager: Smaller Group
1st over 1 year, 2nd over 5 years

Portfolio International Offshore Fund Awards 1996

Bank of Ireland Global Funds offers investors a choice of nine funds, with a minimum investment of just £2,500. If you would like to know more about Bank of Ireland Global Funds, contact

Jonathan Hayes or Tim Phelan
Bank of Ireland Asset Management (Jersey) Limited
Telephone 01534 630888 Fax 01534 630999
Email jhayes4@attmail.com

Bank of Ireland
Asset Management

where basic research is time-consuming and expensive. Most offshore funds have two prices – bid and offer. You buy your units at the higher (offer) price and cash them in at the lower (bid) price. The minimum investment varies: it could be as low as £1,000 while some funds aimed at large investing institutions and backing ultra-specialist areas want £100,000.

Some offshore funds are often marketed under the initials VCIC (Variable Capital Investment Company), SICAV (Société d'investissment à Capital Variable), OEICS (Open Ended Investment Companies) or UCITS (Undertaking on Collective Investment in Transferable Securities). The major difference between them and conventional UK unit trusts is that no tax is deducted at source from your dividends – it is this which makes them the natural home for an expatriate's share-based investments.

Make your next move to Britannia International

If you're living or working abroad, don't forget your money can benefit from a move too. Britannia International offers a range of savings accounts with excellent returns and easy access wherever you are in the world. Our offshore location also enables us to pay interest gross and, as a subsidiary of Britannia Building Society, you have the security of knowing your savings are fully backed by one of the largest building societies in the UK.

For an information pack please call +44 1624 681100.
Alternatively complete and fax or post the coupon below.

Britannia
International

To **Britannia International**   DMMA
Britannia House Victoria Street Douglas Isle of Man IM99 1SD British Isles Fax 01624 681105
Please send me further information on Britannia International accounts.

NAME & ADDRESS

TELEPHONE   FAX

The above information may be used to keep you informed of new Britannia International products and services. If you do not wish to receive this information please tick this box. ☐

FOR A FLEXIBLE RANGE OF COMPETITIVELY PRICED PRODUCTS, TRY THE DERBYSHIRE (ISLE OF MAN) LTD

- Instant Access
- Monthly Income
- 90 Days' Notice
- Bonus Product
- Short Term Fixed Rate Deposits
- Longer Term Fixed Rate Issues

Please 'phone (+44 (0) 1624-663432) or fax (+44 (0) 1624-615133) quoting reference MM for further details

The principal place of business of The Derbyshire (Isle of Man) Ltd (TDIOM) and the office at which deposits are invited to be made is situated in the Isle of Man. The amount of paid up capital and reserves of the company exceed £5.0m. DEPOSITS MADE WITH AN OFFICE OF TDIOM IN THE ISLE OF MAN ARE NOT COVERED BY THE DEPOSIT PROTECTION SCHEME UNDER THE UK BANKING ACT 1987. DEPOSITS MADE WITH AN ISLE OF MAN OFFICE OF TDIOM ARE COVERED BY THE DEPOSITORS COMPENSATION SCHEME CONTAINED IN THE BANKING BUSINESS (COMPENSATION OF DEPOSITORS) REGULATIONS 1991 (REGULATIONS MADE UNDER ISLE OF MAN LEGISLATION). TO FURTHER PROTECT YOUR DEPOSITS DERBYSHIRE BUILDING SOCIETY HAS GIVEN AN IRREVOCABLE AND BINDING UNDERTAKING TO ENSURE THAT WHILST TDIOM REMAINS ITS SUBSIDIARY, TDIOM WILL AT ALL TIMES BE ABLE TO DISCHARGE ITS FINANCIAL OBLIGATIONS AS THEY FALL DUE.

TheDerbyshire

Principal place of business and registered office: PO Box 136, HSBC House, Ridgeway Street, Douglas, Isle of Man IM99 1LR.
Registered with the Financial Supervision Commission for banking business.

Offshore funds come in a huge variety of forms:

- funds which invest in specific stock markets, such as the US, or the Far East. These are riskier than a more general fund which buys into stock markets world-wide.

- so-called umbrella funds, offered by fund management houses and where one fund will have a whole range of specialist sub-funds underneath it. You can usually switch between them if, eg, you decide that the time is right to sell your UK shares and buy into Wall Street. This way, you are not hit by the up-front charge you would pay if you bought into a new fund entirely. One of these funds, Fleming Flagship, based in Luxembourg, has 29 sub-funds covering almost all investment eventualities. Some life insurance firms have taken this concept a stage further by offering you a fund where the sub-funds come from different investment houses, on the principle that a fund manager with an excellent track record in the Far East may not be so good at picking German or French shares.

- currency funds, where you can play the currency markets by investing money into a fund where the managers try to back currencies which are on an up trend. This is a riskier form of investment.

- commodity and futures funds – generally banned in the UK as being too risky, and to be avoided offshore too.

Choosing an offshore fund is difficult simply because of the choice available. This is why it makes sense to find a professional adviser. Funds like these will be a key part of your investment portfolio and so need to be chosen with care.

The best advice is to go for a fund with a broad investment strategy and a consistent reputation for out-performance. Do not be tempted to pile everything into the fund which has produced the best record over the last year – this out-performance is unlikely to be repeated for one of two reasons:

- it reflects either good luck

- or more likely, an investment fashion which will not last. Such fashions have included gold, high technology shares in the US, and shares in Latin American companies, all of which rapidly became money losers.

GILTS AND BONDS

These are a halfway house between cash in the bank and shares. Gilt-edged securities, gilts for short, are basically a loan to the British Government, while bonds are loans to major corporations. Gilts are regarded as being the safest of all investments as the British Government has never reneged upon its debts. Some allow expatriates to receive interest free of tax; those which don't should be avoided.

You can buy gilts through a stockbroker, or from the Bank of England. Some offshore funds specialize in holding gilts and other bonds for the benefit of private investors. As with funds which buy shares, people get a wide spread of risk this way.

The way they work is little understood. Take as an example, the gilt-edged security, 8 per cent Treasury 2013. Holders receive 8 per cent interest each year until 2013, when the gilt is redeemed at par (which is usually £100).

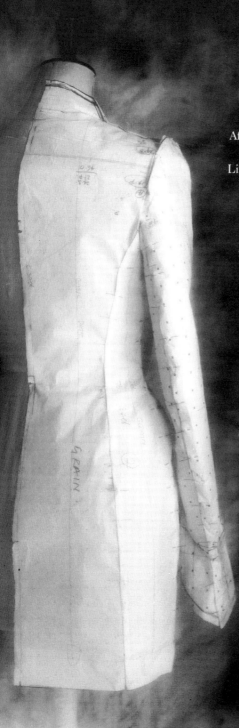

OR
OFF THE PEG?

After a time you appreciate certain things.

•

Like something unique, made to measure.

•

A Private Interest Cheque Account
offering Sterling, U.S. Dollar and
multi-currency cheque books,
free direct debits and standing orders.

•

Lombard lending in 25 currencies.

•

For off the shelf or off the peg,
contact our Private Client
Services department by calling
00 44 (0)1481 723506.
Or fax us on
00 44 (0)1481 720844.

•

Guinness Mahon Guernsey Limited,
PO Box 188, Dept PFME9,
La Vieille Cour,
St Peter Port,
Guernsey, GY1 3LP, CI.

•

Licensed under
The Banking Supervision
(Bailiwick of Guernsey) Law 1994.
Part of the Guinness Mahon
group, wholly owned by
The Bank of Yokohama.
Copies of latest audited accounts
available on request.

GUINNESS MAHON

Guinness Mahon Private Bank

The price on the open market is now £120$\frac{1}{8}$ and will fluctuate until 2013. If interest rates rise, this price will fall; if they fall, it will rise. So gilts offer a secure income if you keep them to maturity, but your capital is at risk if you need to sell before then.

The risk of buying gilts is that inflation might rise, leading to a period of higher interest rates, and so depressing gilt prices, as happened for much of the post-war era.

Bonds work in an identical fashion to gilts with the added risk that even major corporations occasionally default on their bills, although this is extremely rare.

The Bank of England produces a useful booklet on how gilts work (*Investing in Gilts: A guide for the small investor*), available from Public Enquiries Group, Bank of England, 1st floor, Threadneedle Street, London EC2R 8AH.

LIFE INSURANCE

Many of the major UK life insurance firms have set up off-shore subsidiaries to sell their products to expatriates. In many cases, however, these products are not usually a good deal from an investment point of view. The problem is that life-insurance-based investment schemes have to be sold, and as a result, salesmen need to be paid commission to get them to do the selling. This commission has to be paid by you – there's nowhere else it can come from.

And since many people visited by salesmen choose not to buy, those that do buy have the pay for the fruitless calls. To complete the picture, the commission for the life of the policy is paid up-front, and is reclaimed from the first year's contributions.

The risk of buying is therefore that of being locked into a long-term savings contract because you will lose much of your money if you pull out in the early years. This is fine if you know you can stay the course; it is not fine at all if your circumstances change. As a way of making your money grow tax-free, insurance-based schemes compare badly with straightforward share investment schemes such as off-shore funds.

There is a particular danger if you agree to pay regular premiums out of a tax-free expatriate salary when the term of the policy is longer than your contract abroad. When you return to Britain, you may not be able to afford the premiums; surrender the policy and you will make a very poor return indeed. This is an argument for avoiding regular premium contracts; although regular saving in general is a good idea because it is painless and efficient as a way of building up capital, but in this case it leads to inflexibility.

Life insurance works best when it provides simple, no-frills protection policies. This is called term assurance, and pays out a fixed sum if you die during the term. It is excellent sense for people with dependants who might be hard hit financially on death. Expatriates working abroad should check their contract terms carefully – many employers include free life assurance up to certain levels.

PENSIONS

So-called offshore pension plans are heavily marketed to working expatriates, often by salesmen working for life insurance firms. Some are designed to pay out a lump sum, others are structured as a series of plans which pay out each year, effectively giving you an income. While saving for a pension has to be a major priority for anyone not retired, think carefully before you buy. The problem is that in the UK, pensions contributions get tax relief at your highest rate, so that higher rate taxpayers can get £1 into their pension fund by spending 60p. This is a fantastic deal – but as a non-resident, you can't get any tax relief on your contributions. So, in reality, so-called offshore pension plans are really little more than life-insurance-based savings plans, with the risk of buying we discussed above.

There may be marginal tax benefits with some of these plans. The revenue may allow you to take benefits tax-free when you return to Britain in respect of their period built up while you were away; with others, you can transfer the proceeds tax-free into a personal pension which does give you tax relief. Check carefully before you sign up.

HOW TO CHOOSE A FINANCIAL ADVISER

Finding a financial adviser you trust is well worth doing. It matters particularly offshore because you have to live with a factor which is not present in the UK – currency fluctuations. Simply put, if you are living in Spain, your bills will be paid in Spanish pesetas. This can be a problem when the peseta is strong against the pound and your income is paid to you in pounds.

Naturally, it can work the other way too, and the recent strength of sterling has boosted the living standards of many Britons living abroad. But do you want to gamble your lifestyle on the currency markets? A good financial adviser will help you factor this matter into your planning.

Sadly, not all advisers are equal. Each year, the regulators close several down. Good advice is worth paying for and the trend is already there for advisers to be paid on a fee basis, rather than by commission from firms whose products they sell. This is a good idea, as it removes the nagging doubt that an adviser's judgement could be biased by commission. Expect to pay around £100 an hour; it may seem a lot, but if you don't pay for it up-front, you will pay for it in commission. Remember, too, that there are times when the best advice on investments is to do nothing, and someone who has to earn commission has an incentive not to make this clear. Many advisers who charge a fee will rebate the commission they receive to you as a *quid pro quo*. The specialist magazine *Money Management* (see Appendix) has a list of financial advisers who charge a fee.

So when considering someone to look after your financial affairs, there are a number of points you need to ask.

- First, the obvious one. Is he or she really an independent financial adviser? Some sneaky firms of insurance salesmen have called themselves financial advisers, quite legally. But this is not at all the same as a truly independent financial adviser – an insurance salesperson can only sell their own firm's products, not comb the entire market for you.

- Who is the adviser regulated by? Other things being equal, you will get a better deal and have more protection buying from someone regulated by the Personal Investment Authority in the UK, than someone regulated – if at all – elsewhere. You can check the status of an adviser by calling the Central Register, the list of regulated people maintained by the Financial

Supervisory Authority, the successor to the Securities and Investments Board in London. Call 0171–929 3652.

■ Do you feel happy with the adviser? Are your questions answered clearly and sufficiently? Do you have confidence in your adviser in general? Are you made to feel silly if you ask questions which are important to you? If so, find another one. This may be no reflection of the adviser's skill and competence, but in something as sensitive as this, you want someone with whom you are happy dealing, just as you would with a doctor or a solicitor.

■ See the adviser in their office rather than at home if possible – it helps give you a stronger impression of the firm.

■ Ask about experience – how long has he or she been in business? What about qualifications?

■ Then think about the advice you are being given. An adviser should first ask you a lot of detailed questions – about your hopes, aspirations, investments so far, and attitude to risk. As a result a full picture of your affairs should emerge – be sceptical if the adviser does not ask you for enough information to build up a full financial picture.

■ Be sceptical if the adviser recommends that you buy investment bonds issued by insurance companies. These have no real benefits for you, but pay the adviser more commission than would an offshore fund investing in essentially the same thing. Less scrupulous firms of advisers use them a lot.

- Be sceptical too if the adviser recommends an in-house investment scheme called a broker bond. In most cases, these add only an additional layer of charges and, as a result, diminish the value of your money by precisely this amount. Regulators in the UK have been concerned about their sale for some time, and quite rightly so, as they completely undermine the concept of independent and impartial advice. After all, if an adviser also runs a broker bond, its very existence places a great and sometimes irresistible temptation in their path. It is to be hoped that regulators demand that such schemes be shut down.

- Be on your guard if your adviser recommends that you cash in existing investments to buy new ones. This rarely makes sense, and almost never does so with insurance-linked schemes, where you have to stay the full term to get the best return. Unscrupulous advisers can gain substantial commissions this way, and regulators have banned this practice – called churning in the UK. But it still goes on offshore.

- Recommendation from a satisfied customer is always the best way of finding an adviser. If you can't get a recommendation, you may want to talk to two or three before settling on one you feel comfortable with.

- If you want to talk about specialist problems such as trusts or inheritance tax planning, make sure that the adviser you deal with has expertise in that area.

- For greater safety and peace of mind, make your cheque out to the underlying company whose investments you are buying (Sun Life, Prudential, Fidelity, etc), rather than to the adviser himself.

KEEPING IN TOUCH

You will want to monitor your investments on a regular basis, and your adviser may have a regular clients newsletter as well as a yearly or half yearly statement of your portfolio.

The *Financial Times* lists prices for many offshore funds, while two specialist magazines – *Resident Abroad* (see Appendix) and *Investment International* (see Appendix) carry regular investment articles.

The other way of keeping in touch with what is going on is the Internet. The number of people with Internet access is growing exponentially, and most financial services groups have opened up web pages with details of their products and prices which can be accessed from anywhere in the world at any time of night or day. The next step will be to allow people to deal on-line, and the advent of secure encryption technology to defeat hackers will accelerate this process. The Internet also allows people to keep up with the world events which drive the investment market in a way which is not possible for the working expatriate living in an oppressive regime where the press is rigorously censored.

9

HEALTH INSURANCE

THE National Health Service is deservedly called the jewel in the welfare state's crown. Medical help, regardless of who you are, is still largely free at the point of use. While there has been a growth in the popularity of private medical insurance in recent years, most people do not take out this expensive and rarely comprehensive cover, because the National Health Service already provides.

Unhappily, this state of affairs does not always exist abroad. And even if it does, UK expatriates may not be allowed free access to the health service in question. Whether or not you can get any degree of free health care in a particular country will depend on where you are and if the UK has a reciprocal agreement with that country.

If you are not covered by your host country's health care system, then expensive private medical insurance may have to be the order of the day, as otherwise the alternatives are either to forego treatment or face spiralling medical bills for it.

Similarly, there is a very good chance you will not qualify for other social security benefits from your host country. This includes not only unemployment benefits, but maternity cover, industrial injury payments, statutory sick pay and a host of other benefits.

The good news is that at least some of these benefits are portable if they are already in payments at least for a short time. This means you do not necessarily lose a benefit in payment immediately if you go abroad.

HEALTHCARE AGREEMENTS ABROAD

European Union countries and those in the European Economic Area as well as some non-European Union countries have reciprocal health care agreements with the UK. This will give you a measure of free medical cover while you are abroad.

But do not assume that all the benefits you take for granted from the National Health Service will be on offer in exactly the same way. You may well find that there are significant gaps in what your host country's health system provides and you may have to buy private medical insurance to cover such gaps.

Despite years paying taxes to fund the National Health Service, you may find you are off to a country that will not bale you out if you have a medical crisis. But you cannot get any of the money back you have paid into the National Health Service even if you have rarely used it and going abroad will mean you never claim it in the future.

If you go to work in a European Economic Area country, you will have some degree of cover, but this may well depend on your having already contributed to the UK's social security system. The European Economic Area countries are: Austria, Belgium, Denmark, Finland, France,

Wherever

The standard of healthcare varies enormously from country to country – as does the cost. But wherever you are, you can enjoy quality healthcare without the wait, the worry and the cost with the PPP healthcare International Health Plan.

you are in the world,

Exclusively for people living, working or travelling abroad, it gives you access to private treatment, annual cover of up to £1 million per year and a 10% discount for the length of your membership.

we're there

There's also a 24-hour Health Information Line to answer any health – related queries, your own Personal Advisory Team to resolve any other questions and, in medical emergencies, a fast evacuation and repatriation service.

to support you.

To find out more about the PPP healthcare International Health Plan, or for a no-obligation quotation or even immediate cover, contact us today on the numbers below or complete and return the coupon.

+ 44 (0) 1323 432002

Or fax the coupon below on +44 (0) 1323 432785. Please quote reference: ME1126

Please send me further details about the PPP healthcare International Health Plan and a quotation.. Post to: PPP healthcare, PPP house, Upperton Road, Eastbourne, East Sussex BN21 1BR UK.

Mr/Mrs/Miss/Ms	Surname
Forename	
Address	

Postcode	Principal country of residence
Tel. No.. Day	Evening
Fax No.	Date of birth / /

Your partner's date of birth   /   /

No. of children under 21 ☐

Area in which you require cover   Worldwide ☐

Worldwide excl. USA/Canada ☐   Europe inc. UK ☐

(Important : we cannot give you a quotation without your date of birth.)
If you would also like details of our International Health Plan for Companies, please tick here ☐
If you intend spending most of your time in any of the following countries, please tick the relevant box: UAE ☐ Cyprus ☐ Malta ☐
Reference: ME1126

PPP healthcare™

there to support you.

Germany, Greece, Iceland, Italy, Liechtenstein, Luxembourg, Holland, Norway, Portugal, Republic of Ireland, Spain, Sweden and the UK. If you fall ill in one of these countries you may need to prove that you have actually paid in to the UK's social security system. To do this, you need to get hold of a Department of Social Security form E104 from the Contributions Agency (see Appendix). This will detail when you have paid into the UK's state social security scheme.

To get health care in the country you are living in, get a copy of form E111 from your local Post Office. You must take this form with you. If you fall ill and use medical facilities that you have to pay for, you cannot later fill out the form and claim back the money you have already spent. If you go overseas and are either self-employed or work for a company in that country, you may find yourself paying into that country's social security insurance scheme. In some of these countries the self-employed or employed workers earning over a certain amount do not have to pay into these schemes. If this is an option, take care you do not find yourself and your dependants without any cover at all. These amounts you have saved may be swallowed up by unforeseen and massive medical bills.

Unusually Gibraltar, which is normally regarded as part of the UK when it comes to benefits overseas, falls outside this network. The Rock has a completely different way of paying for its health care system. You can only get emergency treatment for up to 30 days if you fall ill there, thanks to a special agreement with the UK. The only way around this is to join and start paying into the Gibraltar Group Practice Medical Scheme. Other countries also have healthcare agreements with the UK. These agreements will give

Simply the best health insurance money can buy

Over the years International Health Insurance danmark a/s has incorporated all the elements demanded by people who, when it comes to matters of health, need the ultimate protection.

By listening to our clients, and closely monitoring all their health needs when they're away from home, we are able to respond with plans to suit each and every individual.

Get more information about the most important card in your and your family's life – fill out the coupon today and discover how the world's best health insurance can help you to face the future with confidence.

The card that gives credit to your health

International Health Insurance danmark a/s

Name.. Age ....
Address..
Postal Code................................City ....
Country ....
Tel. ....
Nationality ....

International Health Insurance danmark a/s
64a Athol Street, Douglas, Isle of Man, British Isles IM1 1JE
Tel.: +44 1624 677412, Fax: +44 1624 675856

you access to at least some of those countries' healthcare benefits for free or at a subsidized rate.

However, once again, do not assume that it will mirror the help available from the National Health Service. It is a very good idea to double check what is and is not on offer and use private medical insurance to mend any holes in the safety net.

Countries with reciprocal healthcare agreements with the UK are: Australia, Barbados, some British Dependent Territories, Anguilla, British Virgin Islands, Falkland Islands, Hong Kong, Monserrat, St Helena and the Turks and Caicos Islands.

Also included are: Bulgaria, the Channel Islands, the Czech and Slovak Republics, Gibraltar, Hungary, the Isle of Man, Malta, New Zealand, Poland, Romania, some ex-USSR republics – Armenia, Belarus, Azerbaijan, Georgia, Kazakhstan, Kirgizstan, Moldova, Russia, Tajistan, Turkmenistan,

Private Medical Insurance that makes time stand still

Just take a moment to consider this.

If you commence your private medical insurance with Exeter Friendly Society at say 40, you'll pay the subscriptions of a 40 year old for life. How many other private medical insurers make you such an offer?

You see, at Exeter we never increase your subscriptions simply because you get older, which can save huge amounts over the years. Because we are a friendly society, with no shareholders to pay, all surpluses are utilised to improve benefits for Members.

For full details, please telephone, fax or return the coupon.

WE MAKE YOU FEEL SO YOUNG

Subscriptions will increase to reflect rising costs of treatment and developments in medical expertise and technology.

80
70
60
50
40
30

If you are under 76 years of age please telephone **+44 1392 477210**, fax **+44 1392 477235** or complete this coupon for details.

Mr/Mrs/Ms _____

Address _____

_____

_____ Tel: _____

Ages of people to be included _____

Current insurer _____ Renewal date _____

inter PLAN **EXETER** FRIENDLY SOCIETY

MA 01/97

BEECH HILL HOUSE, WALNUT GARDENS, EXETER DEVON EX4 4DG

Your Prescription for
Cost-Effective Cover Abroad *ExpaCare*
Protection for Expatriates

✂ -

Please send me the ExpaCare International Health Health Plan brochure

☐ **Individual**   ☐ **Group** *(minimum of 5 employees)* please tick

Name ....

Nationality .... Age ....

Address ....

....

Country of Residence ....

Mail to: **ExpaCare**, Dukes Court, Duke Street, Woking, Surrey GU21 5XB, England   **RA 6/97**
Tel: +44 1483 717800 Fax: +44 1483 776620

For further information **please insert 6447** on Reader Enquiry Card.

Ukraine and Uzbekistan. Countries that make up the former Yugoslavia – Serbia, Montenegro and the successor states of Croatia, Bosnia-Herzegovina, Slovenia and the former Yugoslav republic of Macedonia – are also included.

If you go to live and work in any country not listed here, you get no help whatsoever if you have an accident or fall ill. If this is the case, then you should really take out private medical insurance to cover you instead.

PRIVATE MEDICAL INSURANCE

Private medical insurance has the reputation of being some-thing of a luxury in the UK, an optional extra for people unwilling to wait their turn in a National Health Service queue for treatment. But if you find yourself stranded abroad ill and with no access to state healthcare, then it suddenly becomes one of life's necessities.

If you are lucky, your overseas employer will pay for your private medical cover for you as a perk of the job. If not, the onus is on you to buy the cover for both yourself and your family. Private medical insurance does not effectively replace the state healthcare system. Most policies carry with them sets of exclusions for pre-existing illnesses and other problems. What you get will largely depend on how much you are prepared to pay out in premiums each month or year. The more you pay, the better the cover. So make sure you know exactly what you are getting before you sign on the dotted line.

For example, BUPA International, the overseas arm of the UK's biggest private medical insurer has a list of nine areas it will NOT pay out on:

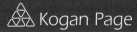

- pre-existing conditions. If you have suffered an illness such as cancer and it comes back, then there will be no pay out for treatment. Depending on which insurer you go with, the pre-existing condition exclusion usually lasts from two to five years.

- convalescence

- pregnancy and childbirth, fairly important benefits for families living and working abroad

- routine dental cover

- treatment for AIDS or HIV-related conditions which originated during the first five years you had the policy

- cosmetic surgery or treatment

- war risks

- mental conditions arising within the first two years of your taking out the plan

- treatments at health hydras and nature cure clinics.

If you are caught out by any of the nine clauses, you will have to rely on what the healthcare system of that country provides, your employer's largesse or ultimately your own savings.

As well as excluding a range of problems for cover, health insurers basically want to pay out for problems that are short-lived. They do not see their job as replacing long-term in- or out-patient care using the private sector. PPP Healthcare, another of the UK'S major medical insurers, spells this out very clearly in its brochures. It says: 'We pay for illnesses that respond quickly to treatment in the short term. Long-term control of illness is outside the scope of our agreement with you.' There is absolutely nothing wrong with this attitude. But you must be aware of it when you take out your policy. Most private medical insurers include so-called medical evacuation cover, so if you do fall ill, you will be whisked back to the UK where you can at least get treatment.

Private medical cover can be expensive and the costs rise as you get older and inevitably fall prey to more illnesses. But it is worth asking yourself if you can afford to pay out extra as it will give you far more protection.

While all of BUPA's three-level types of plans all have maximum annual cover of up to £500,000 and full refund for medical evacuation cover, what they look after you for elsewhere varies greatly (see Table 9.1). Its more comprehensive Classic

Table 9.1 Table of annual costs for world-wide policies excluding cover in the USA and Canada

Age	Essential	Classic	Gold
Under 21	£184	£236	£291
21–24	£267	£343	£426
25–29	£349	£448	£569
30–34	£380	£486	£618
35–39	£409	£536	£668
40–44	£475	£609	£762
45–49	£556	£719	£895
50–54	£607	£786	£999
55–59	£730	£946	£1,216
60–64	£943	£1,209	£1,570
65–69	£1,367	£1,753	£2,277
70–74	£1,593	£2,042	£2,704
75–79	£1,861	£2,317	£3,071
80-plus	£2,104	£2,698	£3,505

Further Kogan Page titles...

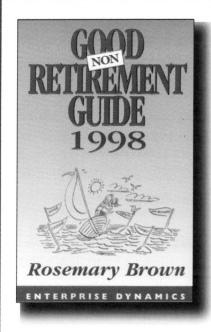
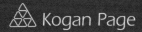

and Gold plans pay for out-patient fees of up to £2,000 a year for things like acupuncture, osteopathy, chiropractic and homeopathy, but the basic Essential plan does not. Only the Gold plan allows for primary consultations and primary care which includes prescribed drugs up to £600 a year.

Private medical insurance plans that include cover in the USA and Canada are noticeably more expensive because of spiralling health costs. Don't forget legal costs are forcing up the cost of health care in North America. Anyone over 65 years old seeking cover is individually assessed if they intend to live in either country.

OTHER STATE BENEFITS ABROAD

A number of UK social security benefits can be paid to you while you are abroad, at least in the short term. Some of these depend on how much National Insurance you have paid, while others do not.

Unlike the basic State pension and widow's benefits, you cannot use voluntary Class 3 National Insurance contributions to ensure you get your maximum benefit entitlement when you retire or claim (see Chapter 6).

There is a range of benefits that depend on the National Insurance contributions paid while you lived and worked in the UK.

■ Incapacity benefit comes in three levels: the short-term lower rate of £47.10 a week in the 1997–98 tax year for the first 28 weeks, the higher rate for weeks 29 to 52 of £55.70 a week and long-term incapacity benefit of £62.45 a week.

   If you qualify for this benefit, you can be paid it for

the first 26 weeks abroad if you are going abroad temporarily for medical treatment or have been incapable of work for the last six months. The long-term benefit may be paid for longer than 26 weeks. Get form BF5 from your local Social Security office for details.

- Maternity benefits. Women in the European Economic Area qualify for statutory maternity pay of a minimum of £55.70 for six weeks, or maternity allowance of at least £48.35 for 18 weeks. You can get these benefits for up to 26 weeks – again, if your absence is temporary and you are either going for treatment or have been unable to work for the previous six months.

- Jobseeker's allowance. It is important to remember that National Insurance contribution-related Jobseeker's allowance cannot usually be paid to you outside the UK.

Some other benefits that do not rely on a National Insurance track record can also be paid if you are abroad, usually in another European Economic Area country, if your stay is temporary and you are there either for medical treatment, or you have been unable to work for the previous six months. If you are going to claim, you must tell your Social Security office before you leave. These other benefits are:

- attendance allowance at least £33.10 a week in 1997–98.

- disability working allowance – the amount depends on individual assessment – will only be paid abroad if you left when payment had already started and stops at the end of its 26-week payment period.

- child benefit, starting at £11.05 a week in 1997–98 for the eldest child, will only be paid for the first eight weeks of a temporary absence. If you go abroad permanently, the child benefit stops.

■ industrial injuries benefits. Provided your disability is the result of working in the UK, you can claim up to a maximum of £101.10 a week in 1997–98, and these benefits can be paid out to you if you are living overseas.

■ statutory sick pay. If you work for a UK employer in the European Economic Area that pays Class 1 National Insurance contributions, you may be able to claim statutory sick pay from your employer. This is up to £55.70 a week in 1997–98.

For details of what benefits you can and cannot claim outside the UK, get the booklets NI 38 *Social Security Abroad* and SA29 *Your Social Security Insurance, Benefits and Health Care in the European Community* from your local Social Security office.

10

COMING HOME

GOING abroad does not mean making a permanent break with the UK. Quite apart from leaving family and friends, expatriates leave behind them mortgages, possessions, private pensions, all the benefits built up after paying years of National Insurance and private pension contributions. Whether working abroad or retiring to that place in the sun, there is a very good chance you will want to return home, either to retire or, less happily, to get healthcare not available or too expensive in your adopted country.

PAYING THE MORTGAGE

Your biggest asset, retired or working, is your home. The mortgage is most people's biggest monthly commitment and falling behind in the payments not only damages your credit record, but jeopardizes your comfortable retirement home.

If you decide not to sell your home before going abroad, then you have to keep up the payments on it. Once you no longer live there, your monthly payments will inevitably rise. Mortgage Interest Relief At Source (MIRAS) is a tax relief given to domestic mortgages. But the tax relief on interest payments of 10 per cent is only available on what the Inland Revenue calls your principal residence – where you usually live in the UK. Once you leave the UK, you lose this tax relief. While it has been worn away over years by successive tax cuts, it is still worth something.

With MIRAS the monthly mortgage payments on a £80,000 house with an interest-only mortgage, assuming a standard mortgage rate of 8.7 per cent, is £547 a month. Without MIRAS, this rises to £558 a month. The difference is not huge, but as mortgage rates rise, it becomes ever bigger.

Many homeowners lock themselves into special mortgage deals that either guarantee the interest rate they pay will be a set percentage below the standard variable mortgage rate for a set number of years, or they take out a fixed rate mortgage. These fixed rate deals guarantee that the interest rate paid will stay at a set level for the life of the special mortgage deal. These special deals are very attractive for people wanting certainty over their mortgage payments. It is possible to fix your payments for 5, 10, 15 or even 25 years. Although you may lose your MIRAS relief, you will still know how much your monthly payments will be and can budget accordingly.

For people working abroad and paid in a foreign currency, this can be a very good move. Mortgage interest rates rise and fall, and the prospect of rising rates just at the time your currency is losing value against sterling is a scary one. Your foreign currency salary will be able to buy far less just at the time you need to use it to pay more out on your home loan.

While fixing the payments on your home loan does have its attractions, there are dangers too. Fixing into a set interest rate means taking a bet on what the average rates are likely to be over the period of the fix. If you are locked into too high a rate, then you may lose out as you could have paid far less in mortgage payments over the fixed rate period.

This interest rate risk rises the longer you fix your payments for as the gamble on long-term interest rates grows. Unfortunately you cannot simply switch out of these special deals when the going gets a bit tough. Lenders have to buy set amounts of money to fund fixed rates on the international money markets. If borrowers simply upped sticks and cashed in the mortgages, then lenders would lose money.

To stop this happening, lenders impose penalties for cashing in these loans early. Getting rid of the special mortgage deal for at least the life of the fix and often for a couple of years beyond it usually incurs early redemption penalties. These average six months' gross interest or 5 per cent or 6 per cent of the value of the loan. Fixing into a special deal may be a good move, but do take care as it can be a costly gamble that is hard to get out of.

RENTING OUT YOUR HOME

A popular way of keeping up the payments on a home in the UK while abroad is to rent it out. A judiciously set level of rent can cover not only the mortgage payments, but the cost of insurance and any bills that result from the inevitable wear and tear that comes from daily living. But there is a dark side to renting out a property. The wrong tenant can cause you months if not years of misery. Damaged property, alienation of what were once friendly neighbours as a result of noise and bad behaviour, as well as mounting arrears as the rent is not paid are sadly all too common problems. Although the law has recently changed to make it easier to evict such problem tenants, landlords also have legal duties to ensure that homes they rent out are safe and habitable.

If you decide to let out your home, use a professionally qualified letting agent. Surveyors with the Royal Institution of Chartered Surveyors (see Appendix) and management agents registered with the Association of Residential Letting Agents (see Appendix) all have to meet minimum standards as well as have professional indemnity insurance that will pay out if they are found to be negligent. They will also help you set a reasonable level of rent. It needs to cover not only today's monthly mortgage bill, but any potential interest rate rises, insurance, and of course, their slice of your cake.

Property managers cost money, perhaps as much as 10 per cent to 20 per cent of the money you get in rent, but they can be invaluable. They will be able to ensure the lease is properly drawn up – if it is not, then unscrupulous tenants may get extra rights that make them next to impossible to evict – and they can check that the property is looked after, repairs made and the rent paid on time.

Resist the temptation to get a friend or relative living near the property to act as managing agent for you. It is an absolute recipe for disaster. With the best will in the world they will not have the expertise for the job and your friendship may end in a welter of recriminations. Most homes are now let out on assured shorthold tenancies. These allow the tenant to give notice before they have lived in a property for less than six months. But it also allows landlords to set up leases for as short a period as three months.

A recent change in the law also means that if your tenant falls into at least eight weeks' worth of arrears you can start moves to evict them. Before the end of February 1997, land-lords had had to wait 12 weeks before beginning eviction proceedings.

It is very important to make sure the property is up to scratch before you let it out. Poorly maintained homes not only lose value, they also can be death traps for those living in them. This applies not only to the fabric of your home, but to furnishings and appliances too. In general, properties must measure up to the 1991 Building Regulations. So buildings must have a safe means of escape in case of fire and new homes need to be fitted with smoke alarms.

Gas appliances have to be checked at least once a year by a Corgi-registered firm and the tenant has to be given a cer-tificate showing the annual check has been carried out and it is satisfactory. Furniture has to pass flammabilty tests. You could find yourself in the difficult and potential costly position of having to replace family furniture because it does not meet fire regulations.

There is good news on the insurance front if you let out your home furnished. The cost of buildings and contents insurance does not necessarily go up and your policy may be able to be converted automatically to cover the property while you are abroad. For example, Norwich Union does not increase premiums on home insurance when the property owner goes overseas and lets it out. Contents cover includ-ing accidental damage for up to £40,000 in Surrey comes in at £300 a year if you are in the country or not. However, the way the policy works has changed. The policy will now exclude claims for malicious damage or thefts by the ten-ants or the tenants' friends. The only theft claims that will succeed are ones where there has been violent or forcible entry to the property.

SELLING UP

The hassle of keeping up a home in the UK may lead you to decide to sell it. There should be no problems here. Simply instruct your solicitor and estate agent in the UK and they will do it for you.

Provided the property is still your principal residence in the UK and you had intended to return to it, the money you get from the sale should not be hit by capital gains tax. This is important, as capital gains tax is charged on any such large capital gain you make over £6,500 in the tax year 1997–98. Any gain over that £6,500 gets taxed at between 20 per cent and 40 per cent if the house is not your principal residence.

PROTECTING YOUR PENSION

Everyone builds up pension benefits throughout their working lives whether they know it or not. The simple fact of paying National Insurance contributions means that you are building up your State pension, while most employers still offer some form of company pension scheme that most employees are well advised to pay in to.

You do not lose your pension rights when you go abroad. The pensions built up by that time are protected to some extent. However, you may find that you cannot continue building them up while overseas.

The State pension, relying as it does on National Insurance contributions, will not increase in size if those contributions stop. Employed people paying Class 1 contributions will have to keep up those payments for the first year they are abroad, so to that extent the pension is protected. After that year is up, if you qualify (see Chapter 6 on pensions), you can elect to pay Class 3 voluntary National Insurance contributions. These will allow you to continue to build up your UK State pension, the basis of most people's retirement income.

Employees in company pension schemes may be able to continue paying into their UK pensions schemes while working abroad. Even if this is not the case, your final salary company pension scheme benefits are safe. Since 1985 legislation has come in to make sure the money left by ex-employees in company pension schemes does not wither on the vine. Schemes have to increase these frozen pensions by the rate of inflation up to a ceiling of 5 per cent. This is not perfect, but it does give your pension some protection from the ravages of inflation.

Anyone with frozen company pension scheme benefits put into the deep freeze before 1985 will find that although their pension is not up-rated in line with inflation, it will have been invested so that it does not actually reduce. But in real terms inflation will have eroded your retirement income significantly, so make sure you have made alternative provisions. Your personal pension should also be safe. Although no more money is paid in, the insurance company running it will continue to manage it and hopefully make your pot of money grow. The only potential problem here is if you are invested in a badly run fund that does not perform well. Check with your personal pension company that you will not be charged extra for stopping payments into your fund. If this is the case, talk to an independent financial adviser about whether it is a good idea to shift your money to a company that does not make such swingeing charges before you go abroad.

When you return to the UK to retire there should be no

problem about these State and private pensions being paid. Remember to keep a record of your National Insurance number with your policy documents so when you do return there are no problems about claiming your rightful benefits.

OTHER RECORDS

Once you have told the Department of Social Security you are going overseas, a chain of events begins that can often end up with your medical records being destroyed. This can cause problems later on when you return to the UK. It is possible to prevent this problem occurring in the first place.

When you tell the DSS Contributions Agency you are off, it has to tell the National Health Service Central Register, which then amends its Central Index of Patients. It has to do this as the funding given to each Family Health Service Authority is worked out on the number of patients it has.

The FHSA, basically the medical equivalent of your local council, will withdraw your records from your GP about nine months after you have gone abroad. It will hang on to your medical records for six years and then it will destroy them. This will cause problems when you get back, not least if you want life insurance but cannot prove your past good health.

To stop this situation arising, tell your GP when you are going and when you intend to return. This way, your medical records will not be withdrawn from your GP's files unnecessarily. Tell your GP you are back as soon as you return, so your files can be kept in his or her files and not withdrawn and destroyed by mistake simply because your GP and FHSA think you are still abroad.

APPENDIX –
USEFUL ADDRESSES

Allied Pickfords, Heritage House, 345 Southbury Rd, Enfield, Middlesex EN1 1UP. Tel: 0800 289229

Association of Residential Letting Agents, Maple House, 53–55 Woodside Rd, Amersham, Bucks HP6 6AA.

Bank of England, Public Enquiries Group, 1st Floor , Threadneedle Street, London EC2R 8AH. Tel: 01494 431 680

Benefits Agency, Pensions and Overseas Benefits Directorate, Department of Social Security, Tyneview Park, Whitley Road, Benton, Newcastle upon Tyne NE98 1BA. Tel: 0191 218 7777

Bennett & Co., 39 London Road, Alderley Edge, Cheshire SK9 7JT. Tel: 01625 586 937

Blackstone Franks, Barbican House, 26–34 Old Street, London EC1V 9HL. Tel: 0171 250 3300

British Association of Removers, 3 Churchill Court, 58 Station Road, North Harrow, Middlesex HA2 7SA. Tel: 0181 861 3331

BUPA International, Russell Mews, Brighton BN1 2NR. Tel: 01273 323 563

Centre for International Briefing, The Castle, Farnham, Surrey GU9 0AG. Tel: 01252 721 194

Companies House, Offices in London, Cardiff, Edinburgh, Birmingham, Manchester, Glasgow and Leeds.
Tel: (London) 0171 253 9393; Cardiff 01222 380 801
Web Site www.Companies-house.gov.UK

Conti Financial Services, 204 Church Road, Hove, East Sussex BN3 2DL. Tel: 01273 772 811

Contributions Agency, International Services, Longbenton, Newcastle upon Tyne NE98 1YX. Tel: 06451 54811 or
0191 225 4811

Cornish & Co., Lex House, 17 Hainault St, Ilford, Essex IG1 4EL.
Tel: 0181 478 3300

Department of the Environment, Transport and Regions, Blackhorse Road, London SE99 0TT.

Disability Working Allowance Unit, Department of Social Security, Freepost (PR1211), Preston PR2 2TF.

Employment Conditions Abroad, Anchor House, Britten Street, London SW3 3TY. Tel: 0171 351 5000

148

European Council of International Schools, 21b Lavant Street, Petersfield, Hants. Tel: 0173 268 244. www.ecis.org

Federation of Overseas Property Developers, Agents and Consultants, PO Box 3534, London NW5 1DQ. Tel: 0171 836 9524

Independent Schools Information Service, 56 Buckingham Gate, London SW1E 6AG. Tel: 0171 630 8793. www.isis.org.UK

Investment International, 4–8 Tabernacle Street, London EC2 4LU. Tel: 0171 638 1916

Law Society, 50 Chancery Lane, London WC2A 1SX. Tel: 0171 242 1222

Law Society of Scotland, 26 Drumsheugh Gardens, Edinburgh EH3 7YR. Tel: 0131 226 7411

Money Management, 149 Tottenham Court Road, London WIP 9LL. Tel: 0171 896 2525

Portuguese Chamber of Commerce, 1–5 New Bond Street, London W1Y 9PE. Tel: 0171 494 1844

PPP Healthcare, Phillips House, Crescent Road, Tunbridge Wells, Kent TN1 2PL. Tel: 01892 512 345

Resident Abroad, 149 Tottenham Court Road, London W1 9LL. Tel: 0171 896 2525

Royal Institution of Chartered Surveyors, 12 Great George St, Parliament Square, London SW1P 3AD. Tel: 0171 222 700

Social Security Agency, Contribution Unit Headquarters, International Services, 24–42 Corporation Street, Belfast BT1 3DP. Tel: 01232 251411.

Timeshare Council, 23 Buckingham Gate, London SW1E 6LB. Tel: 0171 821 8845

The Women's Corona Society, Commonwealth Institute, Kensington High Street, London W8 6NQ. Tel: 0171 610 4407

INDEX

Page references in *italic* indicated tables

Index of advertising